Narr

at is the role of narrative in how people learn throughout their lives? Are there different
ns and forms of narrativity? How do they influence learning?

d on data gathered for the *Learning Lives* project, which sought to understand learn-
questioning individuals about their life stories, this book seeks to define a new learn-
eory which focuses on the role of narrative and narration in learning. Through a
er of detailed case studies based on longitudinal interviews conducted over three-
ur-year periods with a wide range of life story informants, *Narrative Learning* high-
ghts the role of narrative and narration in an individual's learning and understanding of
v they act in the world. The authors explore a domain of learning and human subjectiv-
ity which is vital but currently unexplored in learning and teaching and seek to re-position
learning within the ongoing preoccupation with identity and agency. The 'interior conversations' whereby a person defines their personal thoughts and courses of action and creates
their own stories and life missions, is situated at the heart of a person's map of learning and
understanding of their place in the world.

The insights presented seek to show that most people spend a significant amount of time
rehearsing and recounting their life story, which becomes a strong influence on their
actions and agency, and an important site of learning in itself. *Narrative Learning* seeks to
shift the focus of learning from the prescriptivism of a strongly defined curriculum to
accommodate personal narrative styles and thereby encourage engagement and motivation
in the learning process. Hence the book has radical and far-reaching implications for existing governmental policies on school curriculum.

The book will be of particular interest to professionals, educational researchers, policy
makers, undergraduate and postgraduate learners and all of those involved with education
theory, CPD, adult education and lifelong learning.

Ivor F. Goodson is Professor of Learning Theory at the Education Research Centre,
University of Brighton, UK.

Gert J. J. Biesta is Professor of Education at the Stirling Institute of Education, University
of Stirling, UK.

Michael Tedder is an honorary Research Fellow in the Graduate School of Education,
University of Exeter, UK.

Norma Adair is a former Research Fellow at the Education Research Centre, University
of Brighton, UK.

Narrative Learning

Ivor F. Goodson, Gert J. J. Biesta,
Michael Tedder and Norma Adair

 Routledge
Taylor & Francis Group

LONDON AND NEW YORK

First published 2010
by Routledge
2 Park Square, Milton Park, Abingdon, Oxon OX14 4RN

Simultaneously published in the USA and Canada
by Routledge
270 Madison Avenue, New York, NY 10016

Routledge is an imprint of the Taylor & Francis Group, an informa business

© 2010 Ivor F. Goodson, Gert J.J. Biesta, Michael Tedder and Norma Adair

Typeset in Garamond by Swales & Willis Ltd, Exeter, Devon
Printed and bound in Great Britain by
CPI Antony Rowe, Chippenham, Wiltshire

British Library Cataloguing in Publication Data
A catalogue record for this book is available from the British Library

Library of Congress Cataloging-in-Publication Data
Narrative learning / Ivor F. Goodson . . . [et al.].
    p. cm.
    Includes bibliographical references.
    1. Education—Biographical methods. I. Goodson, Ivor.
    LB1029.B55N36 2010
    370.72—dc22
    2009036479

ISBN10: 0–415–48893–1 (hbk)
ISBN10: 0–415–48894–X (pbk)
ISBN10: 0–203–85688–0 (ebk)

ISBN13: 978–0–415–48893–8 (hbk)
ISBN13: 978–0–415–48894–5 (pbk)
ISBN13: 978–0–203–85688–8 (ebk)

'For Martin Bloomer, Committed Educator'

Contents

About the authors

Ivor F. Goodson is currently Professor of Learning Theory at the Education Research Centre, Mayfield House, the University of Brighton, UK. A review of his activities and publications can be found at www.ivorgoodson.com. In addition to his post at the University of Brighton, he is also currently Stint Foundation Professor at the Department of Education, Uppsala University, Sweden and Research Associate at the Von Hugel Institute, St Edmunds College, University of Cambridge.

Gert J. J. Biesta (www.gertbiesta.com) is Professor of Education at the Stirling Institute of Education, University of Stirling, Scotland, and Visiting Professor for Education and Democratic Citizenship at the School for Education, Communication and Culture, Mälardalen University, Sweden.

Michael Tedder spent much of his professional career as a teacher in further and adult education where he had a particular interest in teacher training for the sector. His doctoral research used biographical methods to study Access students and he subsequently worked on two major projects in the Teaching and Learning Research Programme (TLRP), including Learning Lives. He is currently an honorary Research Fellow in the Graduate School of Education at the University of Exeter.

Norma Adair was a Research Fellow at the Education Research Centre, University of Brighton, throughout the data collection period of the Learning Lives project. Dr Adair has considerable experience of teaching, learning administration and management in education and industrial settings, including the development of industry/educational links in Swindon and Wiltshire. She completed her doctoral thesis at the University of Bath in a study entitled 'Fostering a disposition to lifelong learning: people's perceptions and policy assumptions at Key Stage 3'.

Acknowledgements

Narrative Learning is based on research conducted in 'Learning Lives: Learning, Identity and Agency in the Life-Course'. Funded by the Economic and Social Research Council, Award Reference RES139250111, 'Learning Lives' was part of the ESRC's Teaching and Learning Research Programme and was a collaborative project involving the University of Exeter (Flora Macleod, Michael Tedder, Paul Lambe), the University of Brighton (Ivor Goodson, Norma Adair), the University of Leeds (Phil Hodkinson, Heather Hodkinson, Geoff Ford, Ruth Hawthorn), and the University of Stirling (Gert Biesta [Principal Award Holder], John Field, Irene Malcolm, Heather Lynch).

The research team are grateful to the participants for all the information produced, but the interpretations presented in this book are those of the authors alone.

1 Introduction

Life, narrative and learning

The Danish philosopher Søren Kierkegaard has famously said that life must be lived forwards but can only be understood backwards. The question we ask in this book is how people come to develop such understandings and what the significance of such understandings is for how they live their lives. The focus of this book is on stories: on the stories people tell about their lives and the stories they tell about themselves. Such stories are not entirely optional. It is not that we can simply choose to have or not to have them. In a very fundamental sense we exist and live our lives 'in' and 'through' stories. When we are born, we enter into a world full of stories: the stories of our parents, our generation, our culture, our nation, our civilisation, and so on. Over time we begin to add our own stories and through this may alter the stories that have been told about who and what we are. When we die the stories of our lives continue in the stories of others. Stories have the potential to provide our lives with continuity, vivacity and endurance. They can create a past of which we have memories and a future about which we have hopes and fears and can thus bring about a sense of the present in which our lives are lived. Stories can give our lives structure, coherence and meaning, or they can provide the backdrop against which we experience our lives as complex, fragmented or without meaning. Stories do not just provide us with a *sense* of who we are. To a large extent the stories about our lives and ourselves *are* who we are. Where, after all, would we be, and what would we be, without stories?

We tell stories in different contexts and settings, for different reasons and purposes and with different outcomes and effects. Many of our stories are closely interwoven with our everyday lives. They consist of brief exchanges, short anecdotes, things we want to share with others, either for a particular purpose or just for the sake of sharing. Some stories are factual and descriptive; others express our experiences and feelings. And while most stories are about something – an event, an experience, an encounter, a person – they always also express something about ourselves, even if it is only our particular perspective on the situation. Stories serve the purpose of communication;

either communication with others or communication with ourselves, such as in the case of diaries or in our 'internal conversations': our musings, thoughts and daydreams. Sometimes our stories become more reflective and evaluative. This can happen when we begin to ask why certain things in our lives went the way they went, or when we are trying to understand why we acted in a particular way, why we have chosen to do A rather than B, and so on. For some people such reflections come naturally; with others they are triggered by particular events in their lives: by transitions and crises, when normal patterns are interrupted. The stories we construct about ourselves and our lives in such situations can help us to find new meaning and new direction or can support us in coming to terms with the way things are and with who we are. Whilst the way we tell stories is often episodic – focusing on an event or experience – some people develop storylines around which they cluster, relate and re-present the experiences and events of everyday living. Such storylines can become life stories.

The stories we tell about our lives and ourselves can play an important role in the ways in which we can learn from our lives. Such learning, in turn, can be important for the ways in which we live our lives. But the relationship between life, self, story and learning is a complicated one. It is not that the story is just a description of the life and the self, a kind of picture we can look at in order to learn from it. In a very real sense the story *constitutes* the life and the self. Life and self are thus at the same time 'object' and 'outcome' of the story. What complicates the matter further is that the self is also the author of the story. All this means that the *construction* of the story – the *storying* of the life and the self – is a central 'element' of the learning process. In this book we refer to the ways in which we learn from life through storying as *narrative learning* (for this term as initially developed by Goodson and employed herein see Goodson 2006). Narrative learning is not simply learning *from* the stories we tell about our lives and ourselves. It is learning that happens 'in' and 'through' the narration. The stories we tell about our lives and ourselves are therefore to a large extent already the result of such learning processes (see Tedder and Biesta 2009[a]), although it is important to see that in most cases such stories remain unfinished – they are part of ongoing narrative construction and reconstruction.

Since storying is an integral part of how we lead our lives, narrative learning is not necessarily or exclusively a conscious process. Moreover, because stories serve a communicative purpose, narrative learning is often a kind of 'by-product' of our ongoing actions, interactions and conversations. It is only in more exceptional circumstances that we engage deliberately in narrative construction in order to learn from it. This can happen, for example, in adult education programmes that focus on autobiographical work (see, for example, Dominicé 2000; Van Houten 1998; Rossiter and Clark 2007). It can also play a role in forms of psycho-therapy. In this book we are primarily interested in narrative learning as it occurs 'spontaneously', that is, 'in' and 'through' the stories people tell about themselves and their lives without a particular intention to learn from such storying. The stories we present in this book were collected in the Learning Lives project. In this project a group of researchers from the UK conducted repeated interviews with 117 adults aged between 25 and 84 over a three-year period. The interviews were open-ended and used a combination of life-history and life-course approaches in order to gain an understanding of the past and the ongoing present of the participants' lives. All interviews were organised around the simple but crucial question: 'Can you tell me about your life?'

One of the advantages of life *story* research is that it can access the long tradition of work in the life *history* genre, both in the field of adult learning (see, for example, West *et al.* 2007) and in the social sciences more generally (see, for example, Chamberlayne *et al.* 2000). This tradition, with its roots in anthropology, sociology, phenomenology and hermeneutics, has employed life histories as data for over a century. Hence many of the methodological issues have been, if not resolved, at least confronted and discussed (see Goodson and Sikes 2001). The focus of this book, however, is not on life history work as such but on the ways in which people *learn* from their lives 'in' and 'through' the stories they tell about their lives. The focus of this book, in short, is on *learning* and we engage with people's life stories through the lens of narrative. Whereas narrative approaches have been developed and come to fruition in a range of disciplines – including political science, psychology, sociology and economics (see Czarniawska 2004: 3) – there has been relatively little attention to narrative and learning in education and adult education (notable exceptions being Hopkins 1994; McEwan and Egan 1995; and, in the field of adult education, Rossiter 1999; Rossiter and Clark 2007). In North America a good deal of work has focused on the use of narrative in education but without explicit reference to the meaning of the significance of narratives for learning (see Connelly and Clandinin 1990; Clandinin and Connelly 1991). The ambition of this book, therefore, is to cover some new ground through an exploration of the interconnections between life, narrative and learning.

The ideas and insights presented in this book stem from extensive engagement with the data collected through interviews in the Learning Lives project. The stories the participants in the project shared with us were essential for developing our understanding of the relationships between life, narrative and learning. This is why the major part of this book is devoted to the presentation, discussion and analysis of these stories. Even within a book-length account we can only present a small portion of the wealth of material available. We have decided to focus on the stories of eight of the participants in the project, albeit that our understanding of narrative learning has been developed on the basis of the study of a much larger number of participants (see Biesta *et al.* 2008). By confining ourselves to these eight cases we are able to present a more detailed account of the stories and, through this, of the individuals who presented themselves in their stories to us, although even in this way we can still only present a selection of the interview data. The main reason for selecting the eight cases is that they provide the kind of variety needed to develop our argument about the relationships between life, narrative and learning and to present the outlines of our theory of narrative learning. We return to the selection of cases in the final section of this chapter.

The book is organised in the following way. In this introductory chapter we set out the main parameters for our explorations. We start with some information about the Learning Lives project in order to give the reader a sense of the wider context of our work and of some of the methodological aspects of the project. Next we provide a discussion of ideas from narrative theory in order to give a more precise meaning to the notions of 'narrative' and 'narration'. Against this background we then present the analytical framework we will be using throughout this book. This framework focuses on the 'narrative quality' of life stories and life storying and on relationships between narrative quality, learning and action. Our aim has not only been to identify significant differences in the narrative quality of the stories people tell and the storying they are engaged in, but also to get a sense of what people actually do with their stories and storying, both in terms of what they can *learn* from stories and storying and in terms of how this learning may or may not 'translate' into *action*. Our wider ambition has been to develop a theory of narrative learning that brings together the different dimensions of our analysis and sheds light on the different relationships between narrative quality, learning and action. In the concluding chapter of this book we present the outlines of this theory.

Before we start, however, we must make some important provisos. The ambition of this book is to explore the potential of the stories people tell about their lives for the ways in which they might learn from and for their lives. This and nothing more than this is what we aim to do in the chapters that follow. We are therefore not suggesting that people ought to have stories, and even less that they ought to learn from their lives and ought to do so by using stories. We are aware that people can live good, happy and rewarding lives without learning, without stories and without narrative learning. As a matter of fact, in the chapters that follow we will encounter some individuals for whom talking about their life was actually a rather artificial experience, something that didn't come to them naturally. We might therefore compare the stories people tell about their lives to a tool – a tool people can use to learn from and for their lives. Our focus in this book is on the qualities and characteristics of this tool as we aim to understand how stories with different 'narrative quality' allow for different ways of learning and different ways of acting. While it is interesting to ask *why* different individuals tell different kinds of stories and do different things with them, these are not the questions we aim to address in this book. Similarly, there are important sociological questions to be asked about the different ways in which individuals engage with stories, narrative and learning and about the crucial social patterns that can be discerned, but these are also beyond the scope of what we aim to do in this book. The main reason for our focus is that we do not have the data that would allow us to engage with these questions in any depth. Our data, after all, are narrative data, not explicitly at least psychological or sociological data. Our ambition with this book, in other words, is to contribute to the development of a theory of *learning*, not a theory of living.

The Learning Lives project

The individuals whose stories we present and discuss in this book were all interviewed as part of the Learning Lives project, a four-year longitudinal study into the learning biographies of adults. The project was conducted between 2004 and 2008 by a team of researchers from the universities of Stirling, Brighton, Leeds and Exeter. The stated aim of the Learning Lives project was to deepen understanding of the complexities of learning in the life-course whilst identifying, implementing and evaluating strategies for sustained positive impact upon learning opportunities, dispositions and practices and upon the empowerment of adults. More generally our ambition was to investigate what learning 'means' and 'does' in the lives of adults. To this effect we used a broad conception of learning in order to include learning in the context of formal education and work-settings and learning in and from everyday life. Within these different contexts we took a biographical approach (see also Alheit 1995, 2005), focusing on individual adults and their biographies and trajectories, rather than focusing on the characteristics of the institutional contexts.

For the purposes of the project we approached learning as having to do with the ways in which individuals *respond* to events in their lives, often in order to gain control over parts of their lives (see Ranson *et al.* 1996; Antikainen *et al.* 1996; Biesta 2006). Such responses might take a number of quite different forms, ranging from adaptive to more active, creative or generative. To understand learning as having to do with the ways in which people respond to events in their lives implies that it is seen as *contextually situated* (the individual interacting with and participating in the social and cultural milieu) and as having a *history* (both the individual's life history and the history of the practices and institutions in and through which learning takes place). The events to which individuals respond may be *structured* transitions or they may be changes of a more *incidental* nature, including critical incidents such as redeployment or illness. Many such events stimulate encounters with new formal and informal learning opportunities. They can also result in forms of tacit learning of which individuals sometimes only become aware (long) after the event. Learning also occurs, however, in relation to the routines of everyday life, where 'turning points' are not immediately discernible (see also Ecclestone *et al.* 2009).

Over a period of 36 months we conducted a total of 528 interviews with 117 people, 59 male and 58 female, aged between 25 and 84 at the first interview. The average number of interviews was four to five, but in a small number of cases we conducted up to eight or nine interviews. Most interviews lasted for about two hours. The interviews, which used a combination of life-history and life-course approaches, explored the life histories of the participants and tracked their lives over a period of about 36 months. In addition we analysed data from the British Household Panel Survey, an annual panel survey of each adult member of a nationally representative sample of 5,500 British households (comprising approximately 10,000 individuals per wave). Researchers were guided by the research ethics code of the British Educational Research Association. We ensured that participants understood the nature of the research and that they were aware that they could withdraw from the project at any time. We asked for signed consent for participation and the subsequent use of data for academic publication. Participants used self-chosen pseudonyms (except where they insisted on using their own names). We omitted sensitive data where publication might be harmful to participants and anonymised background data in order to protect participants from possible recognition.

The first interviews we conducted with each participant focused on the life history ('Can you tell me about your life?'); subsequent interviews increasingly focused on ongoing events in the lives of interviewees. Interviewers took an open approach, asking for clarification and elaboration, with progressive focusing on key project interests and themes. All interviews were recorded, transcribed and checked by the interviewer. Transcripts were made available to the participants; they were not required to read or check them. In the final interview participants were asked about their experiences of taking part in the project. They were invited to comment on the experience of being asked periodically to talk about their life and, in those cases where they had read transcripts from previous interviews, to comment on that experience as well. A large number of participants indicated that they had 'enjoyed' being interviewed and used positive language about their experience of taking part in the project. There were comments about the process being 'thought-provoking' or giving 'food for thought' and some spoke specifically about reflection and the value found in being given an opportunity to reflect on their experiences with an interested listener.

Responses to the transcripts were more varied. Our approach had been to produce full transcripts that included redundant words and sounds, including hesitation features such as 'ums' and 'errs' and discourse participles like 'you know' or 'I mean', as well as non-syntactical sentences. Indications were also given of pauses and distractions. We found that some of the participants never read the transcripts, whilst others were delighted to have a printed record. Most participants, however, found reading the transcripts an uncomfortable experience – but primarily for reasons of language and grammar than because of content. Several of the participants commented on different kinds of fear that the interviews had generated: fear associated with traumatic experiences recalled from the past; fear of the future; fear that the life portrayed in a transcript appeared boring. Although most had enjoyed the experience, at least one participant said that it was not an experience to be repeated.

The crucial element in our research concerns the ways in which the participants were able to narrate their life story. Such stories are not to be treated as an objective account of the facts of one's life. Life stories are 'lives interpreted and made textual' and should therefore be seen as 'a partial, selective commentary on lived experience' (Goodson and Sikes 2001: 16). Given that the life story is the *current* interpretation of one's past, the way in which a life is storied will crucially depend on the present. The 'now' is, in other words, always present in one's story of the past. This is not to say that each different 'now' will produce a completely different life story. But people do adjust their interpretation and evaluation of their past in the light of new experiences. Current experiences of success, for example, may lead to a quite different account of one's past than current experiences of failure. It is not just the present *situation* which influences one's understanding of the past. The way in which people *understand and articulate* their present situation is important as well. It is, in other words, not just the 'now' that is always present in one's story of the past; it is also one's *story of the 'now'* that impacts on one's story of the past. But just as the present and our understanding of the present influence our stories and interpretations of the past, the past also impacts on the present. Past events do both enable and restrict our opportunities to act in the present. In this respect we can say that the past is present in the 'now'. It is not only the way in which the past enables and restricts what is possible in the present that is important. The past also influences our *understanding* of the present and our ability to articulate and narrate the present, just as our stories of our past and our ability to make sense of our past influence the present and the stories we tell of it. The longitudinal character of the Learning Lives project allowed us to collect stories about the past and stories about the ongoing present. Through this we were able to deepen understanding of the complex interplay of retrospective and contemporaneous dimensions of narrative and narration and it is this which provided us with a unique outlook for the study of learning through the life-course.

Narrative and narration

In his work on narrative, Jerome Bruner (1990) has argued that human beings have two modes of thought or types of cognition or rationality: *paradigmatic* (or *logico-scientific*) *cognition* and *narrative cognition*. Paradigmatic cognition is the process whereby we classify a particular event as belonging to a category or concept and establish the connections between categories and concepts. Such thinking brings order to the complexities of experience by enabling a person to see how individual things belong to categories, what qualities are held in common, and how categories relate to each other. Narrative cognition, on the other hand, starts from the recognition that human action is the outcome of interaction between a person's previous learning and experiences, their present-situated pressures, and their proposed goals and purposes. It focuses on the particular and special characteristics of each action. Narrative cognition is a process through which we can understand the temporal and structural coherence of an individual situated story. Bruner claims that all cultures have such forms of thinking but that different cultures privilege them differently. Western societies in particular have tended to privilege paradigmatic cognition over narrative cognition.

Bruner's views on narrative are closely connected to his notion of 'folk psychology' (see Bruner 1990). Bruner defines folk psychology as 'a set of more or less connected, more or less normative descriptions about how human beings "tick," what our own and other minds are like, what one can expect situated action to be like, what are possible modes of life, how one commits oneself to them, and so on' (ibid.: 35). Folk psychology is related to Harold Garfinkel's notion of 'ethnomethodology' (Garfinkel 1967, 2002) in that it is an approach which focuses on 'the social and political and human distinctions that people [make] in their everyday lives' rather than using 'the classical sociological method – positing social classes, roles, and so on *ex hypothesi*' (Bruner 1990: 37). Folk psychology is thus interested in the *reasons* for human action rather than the *causes* of human behaviour. 'Folk psychology is about human agents doing things on the basis of their beliefs and desires, striving for goals, meeting obstacles which they best or which best them, all of this extended over time' (ibid.: 42–43). Agency is therefore central to folk psychology. 'At their core, all folk psychologies contain a surprisingly complex notion of an agentive Self' (ibid.: 41).

The organising principle of folk psychology is 'narrative rather than conceptual' (ibid.: 35). As Donald Polkinghorne (1995: 5) explains: 'Narrative descriptions exhibit human activity as purposeful engagement in the world. Narrative is the type of discourse composition that draws together diverse events, happenings, and actions of human lives into thematically unified goal-directed purposes.' Whilst acknowledging that there are multiple uses of the term 'narrative', Polkinghorne favours conceptualising narrative as a *story* in which the distinctive feature is a *plot* (see Polkinghorne 1988; see also Brooks 1984; Booker 2004; Ricoeur 1991). A plot serves as 'a type of conceptual scheme by which a contextual meaning of individual events can be displayed' (Polkinghorne 1995: 7).

> Plots function to compose or configure events into a story by: (a) delimiting a temporal range which marks the beginning and end of the story, (b) providing criteria for the selection of events to be included in the story, (c) temporally ordering events into an unfolding movement culminating in a conclusion, and (d) clarifying or making explicit the meaning events have as contributors to the story as a unified whole.
>
> (ibid.: 7)

A plot thus provides temporal structuring and ordering of a story and enables the selection of events for their relevance in the story. However, causal linkages are likely to be recognised only in retrospect and the significance of any particular event may not become evident until a moment of denouement.

Bruner makes a similar point when he emphasises the *sequential nature of narratives*. He explains that 'a narrative is composed of a unique sequence of events, mental states, happenings involving human beings as characters or actors' (Bruner 1990: 43). The constituents of a narrative derive their meaning from the overall configuration of the sequence as a whole, which is the plot of the narrative. The act of grasping a narrative is therefore a dual one: 'the interpreter has to grasp the narrative's configuring plot in order to make sense of its constituents . . .; but the plot configuration must be extracted from the succession of events' (ibid.: 43–44). According to Bruner narratives are also characterised by their *factual indifference*. A narrative can be real or imaginary 'without loss of its power as a story' (ibid.: 44). This is not to suggest that it is impossible to make a distinction between fictional and factual narratives, but rather to highlight 'the structural kinship' between the two forms of narrative (see ibid.: 52).

With regard to the question *why* we construct narratives, Bruner claims that they are only constructed 'when constituent beliefs in a folk psychology are violated' (ibid.: 35). Bruner refers to this as the 'canonical status' of folk psychology, which has to do with the fact that folk psychology 'summarises not simply how things are but (often implicitly) how they should be' (ibid.: 39–40). This means that narratives specialise in 'the forging of links between the exceptional and the ordinary' (ibid.: 47). At the level of cultures Bruner argues that each culture must not only contain a set of norms, but it must also contain 'a set of interpretative procedures for rendering departure from those norms meaningful in terms of established patterns of belief' (ibid.). The function of narratives is precisely '*to find an intentional state that mitigates or at least makes comprehensible a deviation from canonical cultural patterns*' (ibid.: 49–50; emphasis in original).

According to Bruner it is not only at the level of cultures that narratives perform a justificatory role. The same 'quality' can be found at the level of the narratives of individuals, that is, in the stories individuals tell about themselves and their lives. Bruner emphasises that such autobiographical accounts are not simply descriptions of one's life; they rather should be understood as accounts 'of what one thinks one did in what settings in what ways for what felt reasons' (ibid.: 119). Narratives are thus based on the principle of 'justification by exceptionality' (ibid.: 121). They reveal 'a strong rhetorical strand, as if justifying why it was necessary (*not* causally, but morally, socially, psychologically) that the life had gone in a particular way.' (ibid.). The self as narrator therefore 'not only recounts but [also] justifies' (ibid.).

This means that narration is not only about the construction of a particular 'version' of one's life; it is at the same time a construction of (a particular version of) the self. Bruner refers to Polonoff's idea that the self of a life 'is a product of our narrative rather than some fixed but hidden "thing" that was its referent' (ibid.: 112). The self, as Polkinghorne puts it, 'is not a static thing or a substance, but a configuring of personal events into a historical unity which includes not only what one has been but also anticipations of what one will be' (Polkinghorne, quoted in Bruner 1990: 116). Narrating one's life story can therefore be understood as the act of constructing what Bruner refers to as 'a longitudinal version of the Self' (Bruner 1990: 120). Although narratives are constructed, such constructions are not totally free. They are constrained 'by the events of the life' but also 'by the demands of the story the teller was in the process of constructing' (ibid.: 120). At the centre of each autobiography we are therefore likely to find 'a protagonist Self in process of construction: whether active agent, passive experiencer, or vehicle of some ill-defined destiny' (ibid.: 121).

The self is not only the object or product of the narrative but at the very same time the subject of narration. Narratives inevitably have 'something approximating a narrator's perspective' – they cannot be 'voiceless' (ibid.: 77). This is the reason why there is 'something curious' about autobiography in that it is 'an account given by a narrator in the here and now about a protagonist bearing his name who existed in the there and then, the story terminating in the present when the protagonist fuses with the narrator' (ibid.: 121). There is, therefore, a complicated relation between the past, the present and the future in life narratives. Although stories about one's life are about the past, Bruner argues that 'an enormous amount of work is going on here and now as the story is being put together' (ibid.: 122). This is not so much because the narrator needs to work hard to bring events back from memory, but more importantly because in telling about the past the narrator must decide 'what to make of the past narratively at the moment of telling' (ibid.). At the same time there is an orientation towards the future in that the self, as protagonist, is always in a sense pointing to the future. 'When someone says, as if summing up a childhood, "I was a pretty rebellious kid," it can usually be taken as a prophecy as much as a summary' (ibid.: 121).

The foregoing ideas suggest several points that are of relevance for looking at life stories from the angle of narrative. A first point concerns the conceptual distinction between story and narrative. With Polkinghorne we see narratives as stories with a *plot*. Narratives are stories with an organising principle by which the contextual meaning of individual events can be displayed and articulated. Although the emplotment of life events often occurs in a chronological way, it is not a necessary condition for narrative. The presence of a plot is not only important for providing the narrator with a criterion for the selection and organisation of life events. It can also be seen as an indication that someone has learned something from his or her life and, therefore, as evidence of narrative learning (see Tedder and Biesta 2009[a]). A second point has to do with Bruner's suggestion that narratives are never simply descriptive but always also contain an element of justification. Life narratives are constructed, as Bruner puts it, in order to make clear why it was necessary (not causally, but morally, socially, psychologically) that the life has gone in a particular way. Third, although life stories are subjective they are not completely idiosyncratic. Life stories often display formal characteristics of narratives, such as the presence of an actor, action, a goal, a scene and an instrument (Kenneth Burke's so-called 'pentad'; see Burke 1945). More importantly, life narratives often also make use of particular 'scripts', 'archetypes' and 'genres', both with regard to the construction of the story and the construction of the self 'in' and 'through' the story. In this regard Czarniawska (2004: 5) has made the helpful point that the life story (as biography and autobiography) is itself a *genre*; a genre, moreover, with a particular and recent history (the word 'biography' became a recognised term after 1680 while the word 'autobiography' was found in English texts only in 1809). She calls the life story 'one of the most central contemporary genres' and observes that '[i]ts common characteristic is that a narrative of an individual history is placed in a narrative of social history' (ibid.). A final point has to do with the question of the truth of life narratives. According to Bruner the 'power' of the narrative does not depend upon its factual truth so that in this respect narratives are 'factually indifferent.' This is not to say that facts do not matter in narratives. What it does suggest is that what matters in narratives is not simply whether they correspond to reality or not, but how they *function*, both for narrators themselves and in relation to the social settings in which lives are narrated (including interview and research settings).

A framework for analysis

Our focus in this book is on the relationships between life, narrative and learning and, more specifically, on the ways in which people learn 'in' and 'through' their stories and storying. As we have mentioned earlier, we do not see narrative learning as necessarily or exclusively a conscious process. Only a small number of participants did actually identify their storying as a learning process, and even this was more an insight that emerged after a number of interviews than that it was at the forefront of their mind when they joined the project. Nonetheless we found that the stories told contained abundant evidence of learning and of the impact of this learning on people's lives, albeit it a wide range of different ways. We developed our understanding of these processes in a number of steps which eventually became our framework for reading and analysing the life stories. The two main devices we developed for this were the analysis of the *narrative quality* of narrative and narration and the analysis of the *efficacy* of narrative and narration. Within the latter we made a distinction between the learning potential and the action potential of narrative and narration. This has to do with relationships between narrative quality, the ability to learn from narrative and narration and the ability to act upon such learning.

Narrative quality has to do with the significant characteristics of the form and structure of the stories that people tell about their lives. In our analysis we identified five dimensions that we considered important for characterising narratives and narration and for identifying significant differences between different stories and storying. The first three became central to our analysis across cases; the last two highlight aspects that were relevant in relation to some but not all cases. The first dimension is that of *narrative intensity* (Goodson 2010). Narrative intensity not only has to do with the length of the account and the number of words used, but also, and more importantly, with the amount of detail and the 'depth' of the account offered. This is why we characterise the dimension of narrative intensity in terms of *more or less elaborate*. The second dimension of narrative quality concerns the question of whether a story is predominantly *descriptive* or veers more towards *analysis and evaluation*. The question here is whether a story is predominantly an attempt to describe the life, or whether the story can be seen as an attempt to interpret, make sense, and/or evaluate (aspects of) the life. Thirdly, to make sense of one's life – or, to be more precise: to construct a story which presents the life as making sense – is related to the ideas of *plot and emplotment* which have to do with the presence of one or more organising principles within the life story. Although we found some cases where the life story was constructed around a clear plot, more often did we find traces of emplotment, that is, traces of organising and structuring principles within the life narrative. Plot and emplotment are important because they can be taken as evidence that the narrator has come to some kind of understanding of the life, and can thus be taken as evidence of learning – albeit that narrators are not always fully aware of this themselves. In some cases life stories were clearly constructed around key insights and understandings. In other cases we were able to identify underlying themes and structuring principles within the narrative, but we were not always sure whether these also played a role in the perception of the narrators. The fourth dimension of narrative quality has to do with the question of whether the life is recounted in a *chronological or a thematic* way. Although this is a relevant distinction, we found very few non-chronological accounts. We take this as an indication that the most prevalent 'genre' of the life story, at least in the modern Western mind-set, is that of a chronological account (see also Czarniawska 2004: 5). The fifth dimension of narrative quality has to do with the extent to which the narrative is in some way or form *theorised*, i.e., whether the narrator presents us with a theory of life and/or self, or whether the narration veers more towards a *vernacular* account, staying more closely to everyday articulations and understandings. As we will show in the chapters that follow, not all dimensions were to the same extent relevant in reading and understanding the life stories of the participants. Nonetheless, we felt that these five dimensions were the most relevant in characterising the differences between the life stories and in trying to make sense of the interrelationships between life, narrative and learning.

The question of the *efficacy* of life stories has to do with what people can do and actually do in and through their stories and storying. A crucial distinction in this regard is that between the *learning potential* of narrative and narration and the *action potential* of narrative and narration (see also Tedder and Biesta 2009[b]). The learning potential refers to the ways in which and the extent to which people are able to learn from their stories and storying. The action potential has to do with the ways in which and the extent to which such learning 'translates' into action. The learning potential is central to the idea of narrative learning, as it refers to the ways in which and the extent to which the life narrative and the narration of life function as 'sites' for learning. What is particularly important in this regard is the question of the relationship between the narrative quality of life stories and their learning potential. Contrary to our initial expectations, it is not the case that descriptive, non-elaborate narratives do not function as sites for learning whereas analytical and evaluative elaborate narratives do. As we will show in the chapters that follow the correlations between narrative quality and learning potential are more subtle, and of particular significance is the fact that people can be 'caught' in their storying rather than that their storying allows them to generate new perspectives and insights. The other important question has to do with the relationship between learning and action, and thus with the action potential of narrative and narration. One important aspect, as we will show, has to do with the flexibility of narration, that is, with the extent to which narrative and narration can play a role in the ways in which individuals engage with change in their lives. As we will show in the chapters that follow, narrative learning can be an important resource for the achievement of agency (see also Biesta and Tedder 2007), that is, for the ways in which narrative learning translates into or has consequences for the ways in which people live their lives. Our cases show, however, that agency should not simply be equated with the ability to adapt to changing environmental conditions. Agency can also be achieved by resisting such adaptation.

Introducing eight life stories

The main part of this book is constructed around a presentation and discussion of the stories of eight individuals. As mentioned, we have decided to confine ourselves to a small selection of potential cases because we judge that detail is of crucial importance in understanding the relationships between life, narrative and learning. We also judge that coherence matters, i.e., that it is important to get a sense of the life story and the life storying in its full complexity. Selecting the eight cases for this book has not been an easy process, not only because there were so many cases to choose from but also because many other cases bring further refinement and detail to the overall understanding. Our final selection has been based on the extent to which the cases support the development of our theory of narrative learning. This means that we have focused on cases that display different narrative quality and do so with different effects, both in terms of learning and in terms of action. Taken together the eight cases thus shed light on the interrelationships between narrative quality and the efficacy of life narratives and narrations, and thus provide important material for the development of our theory of narrative learning, to which we will return in the concluding chapter of this book.

2   John Peel

We begin our discussion with the story of John Peel. His story provides us with an example of a narrative with relatively low narrative intensity that is more on the descriptive than on the analytical and evaluative end of the spectrum. John's case also provides us with an insight into the conditions under which his kind of narrative can 'translate' into action. It shows us the action potential of relatively stable narratives. John's case also provides us with a healthy reminder that good and fulfilling lives can be lived without much narration and learning.

John Peel

John Peel was born in 1927 in a small hamlet in the south-east of England, the first son and second child of a farmer. John began his formal education at a small town school where he gained almost individual tuition as there were no more than ten pupils in each class. But formal education was never more than a sideshow in John's life. Farming would be and would remain central to his life and to his sense of self. He left the local grammar school aged 15 before taking his school certificates. And just as his parents 'always knew I was going farming' John said that he 'always knew I was going farming' (Interview 2, March 2005). School life always served as a somewhat unwelcome intervention in his life. Commenting on his time at primary school he says:

> . . . I didn't live for it. You know to get home was the main thing and go farming.
>
> (Interview 2, March 2005)

Of grammar school,

> . . . it was something I sort of did, my life was really in the country and getting back farming. That really to me was life.
>
> (Interview 2, March 2005)

... mother always sort of said you know, she'd watch us because ... the station's there and the farm was about a hundred yards up the road and she'd always sort of say, tell me afterwards, you know had seen me come off the train and run all the way, cut up across the fields just to sort of get indoors and changed and get out on the farm, yes, that's all I really wanted to do. Yep. I was lucky.

(Interview 2, March 2005)

By the time John was seven-years-old he was milking cows by hand.

... I was just sort of brought up with them all the time, all free time on the farm, you know either with the men or my father, probably more time with the men I suppose.

(Interview 2, March 2005)

When John was ten-years-old there was an outbreak of Foot and Mouth on the farm and all the cattle had to be destroyed. Christmas 1937 was spent without animals.

My father, always said it was the worst Christmas, he ever had, you know with no animals. Although, a month later, probably about January, whatever it is now, we had the first cattle, bought them again. Which is something I remember as youngsters, we were [coughs] all so excited seeing cattle back on the farm again.

(Interview 1, January 2005)

His father restocked the farm, building up a pedigree herd.

Yes, that's why I've always liked animals and always, just always was part of the farm and part of me, without it, it really wouldn't be farming.

(Interview 1, January 2005)

This does not mean that John *never* considered any other course of action. Briefly, in the war years, he thought about the possibility of the Navy, but without external encouragement this remained just a shadow in his mind.

I suppose it was just stories in those days and various battles and one felt one would like to be part of it, foolishly, but it was the way things were then.

(Interview 2, March 2005)

Instead, John continued to live the 'script' of his birth, having to learn to supervise the German and Italian prisoners of war sent to work on the farm. For about 50 years John continued farming the family farm. There were many changes in this time both in the family structures involved in the farm and in farming more generally, but fundamentally John's life was as his father's had been before him and as he hoped would be for his sons and grandsons in generations to come. It was not to be.

In 1990, disaster struck. There was major flooding in the area and

> . . . a whole lot of salt water, flooded half the farm. It caused us great problems because it killed all the grass and crops where it flooded and to cut a long story short, we had to, have a claim against the Environment Agency, or, I've forgotten who they were at the beginning, but it was something they didn't accept, but it turned out to be part of our life for the next seven years as we fought the case.
>
> (Interview 1, January 2005)

Just as he thought the difficult period was over

> and we thought, right, we should get straight and, sensible again and things will work out, which it did for a year, on and then along came BSE which changed things quite dramatically. The price of the cattle, etc., and then things seemed to go downhill from then, with changing in farming, er as the government, different ideas they had, and sort of not wanting different crops, etc.
>
> (Interview 1, January 2005)

With the spread of BSE disease

> the whole beef industry collapsed which affected the dairy cattle as well because all – a lot of the beef came from the dairy and you know, one, one week your cattle were worth, well up to a thousand pounds, really, eight, nine hundred pounds and then the following week they were worth about two hundred pounds, and commitments we'd made, with the bank and buying various things, you just – you were quite in – had quite a problem with banks.
>
> (Interview 1, January 2005)

In 1995

> we got into a position where, we had to decide and I had to retire or near

retiring and so we sold the dairy herd and the farmhouse where we lived and half, part of the farm.

(Interview 1, January 2005)

Having decided to go into semi-retirement and that the farmhouse and part of the farm had to be sold, John found himself having to deal with the cattle valuers one last time.

> . . . I had a job to talk to them . . .

(Interview 2, March 2005)

One of the valuers, a trainee from New Zealand, empathised, having had a similar experience in his own family. It made John feel 'a bit better'. But emotions were running high. On the day before the sale of the dairy herd:

> . . . we got the cattle in on the, before, the day before the sale, because the sale day they obviously weren't milked, because you sort of just leave them, you know, that morning don't milk them, but the day before it think it took me sort of, well, I just stood with the cows, sort of in the morning, just couldn't let them in. But I was on my own and so nobody saw me. But as I say it still makes me feel, quite, very, emotional I'm afraid. Yes, yep, very emotional.

(Interview 2, March 2005)

> . . . although I helped get ready for the sale, I never went out, [coughs] on the sale day, I just left it to my sons. People came, they were all sold on the farm, but I didn't go out, I kept out of the way.

(Interview 1, January 2005)

Later in the afternoon the land owner from whom John had bought the farmhouse and land and for whom he, and his father before him, had been a tenant for so many years, came to visit John.

> . . . gave me a magnum of champagne. [laughs] He said well it must be the worst day of your life [laughs] which was . . . er . . ., yes, it was. [pause] Yep.
> End of an era.
> Yes. But we've moved on from there.

(Interview 1, January 2005)

As John related the end of his farm as he had known it the pain was tangible, it hung in the air of the dining room where the interview was being held. It was as if John was describing the removal of a vital organ or the amputation of a limb.

Narrative quality

John's narrative is characterised by rather low narrative intensity, at least compared to others in our group. Initially John spoke for about ten minutes before declaring he was 'stuck' and asking for the recording to stop. In the intervening pause, he spoke of his difficulty in telling his life story, partly because of the presence of a recorder, but also because of the 'false' conversation in trying to create a chronological account of one's life to a stranger ('chronological' being John's interpretation of the task). Unlike with others, John's short story did not encapsulate his entire life – he had arrived only at his mid-twenties in a life spanning almost 80 years. He later went on to complete the narration of his life, but it remained somewhat stunted and descriptive in character. There was, so we might say, a certain 'unease' in the telling which seems to suggest that John was unaccustomed to talking about his life and that the telling was relatively unrehearsed.

Although John's narrative veered toward the descriptive end of the spectrum, there were clearly moments of analysis and reflection. When asked, for example, about his motivation for continuing to help out on the farm even after his retirement, he responded:

> I'm sort of one of those foolish people who has to be doing something, you know. You know, people tell me now I shouldn't be working so much, but I enjoy it and I enjoy being with the cattle and so, but, you know, I'm lucky, I'm healthy and I enjoy being with cattle and it's part of my life, and you know, one part's gone but there's another part, something else has sort of moved in, not so good, but, as I say, I've got my health.
>
> (Interview 2, March 2005)

Similarly, when reflecting upon his career as a dairy farmer he said:

> I mean it's still something I miss although, you know we have other animals now, but the dairy cows is, [pause] they're something special. They're not quite like other animals. I mean you handle them every day or twice a day, no, you've just sort of got something with them. Yes. Yep. [pause] It's something gone, I mean I'm very pleased that I sort of did it. Did it for over 50 years. [pause] Yes, it makes me sad now to think of it. Yep.
>
> (Interview 2, March 2005)

John clearly had hoped that the dairy farm would have continued within the family, first by his sons, then by his grandsons.

> . . . at the moment I can't see any grandsons wanting to carry on farming they all seem to, have other ideas, which is really, quite sensible I think nowadays, but um, you know I've got six – six grandsons, and three are one two three yes, yes are grown up as it were, not interested in farming and three you know still might be, you don't know they're young.
>
> (Interview 1, January 2005)

Perhaps the most striking thing about John's narrative is that it centres around a core identity, so we might say, that of being a farmer. We could say that this identity is the organising principle – the plot – in his life story. But less than to think of this plot as the principle through which John is trying to make sense of his life, the identity of being a farmer *is* to a large extent what John's life has been about and what John has been about. In John's case this is not a matter of being 'caught' or 'stuck' in this particular life. It is clear that John very much *wanted* to be a farmer from very early on in his life.

Throughout the period of his working life John had:

> . . . no, real reason for going anywhere, my life was just involved with with the farm and farming and changing times.
>
> (Interview 1, January 2005)

He had no real interest in anything other than

> . . . farming and the country. I didn't really realise there was anything else, actually when I left school. It was only farming I ever wanted to do. [pause] Yes that's all I ever thought of . . . life was really just farming.
>
> (Interview 1, January 2005)

He had spent his working life doing

> . . . what I wanted to do anyway . . . there was no thought of doing anything else. I, I was very happy to go farming . . .
>
> (Interview 2, March 2005)

> . . . working with animals, I suppose. That was sort of my main love really you know just have the dairy cows and working with animals. A farm without animals just wouldn't be a farm, for me.
>
> (Interview 1, January 2005)

Efficacy: Learning potential and action potential

When we ask what kind of opportunities for learning and action John's narrative offers, the first thing to mention is that to a large extent we can see John wanting to stay true to his life as a farmer. In this sense we might say that the story of his life operates as a 'script' and that John's storying follows the script. This is not to suggest that there was no passion for the particular script of John's life or that it was without intrinsic motivation. On the contrary: there is strong personal involvement. Farming was embodied in John and his story speaks strongly to this.

Was there learning in John's life? There probably was. When asked he said:

> . . . as a child, I'm trying to think of some various [pause] things [pause] that suddenly happened and made you learn something, . . . er . . ., no, I suppose I was lucky in life as a young person learning was always quite standard, I didn't have any shocks to learn about life I suppose. I suppose I was brought up in the war and so you sort of learn, actually you did learn about life then, because, you know, friends of yours were killed and I suppose that was all learning. You learnt that life just didn't go on happily and there were always things going wrong. That part of life, really, [pause] and going on into later life I suppose, oh, when one was going out with girls, there again you were learning all the time about other people, other families and other people have got different ideas than you have, and obviously when one gets married, you're learning quite a lot then, about life and other people and children and the effects you have on the children . . . And yes I suppose it's just something that goes on all your life, you just sort of learn things about people, you learn about yourself . . .
>
> (Interview 2, March 2005)

Did his life story play a role in what he learned from life? Was his life story a resource for learning? Probably less so. There is some evidence in the interviews of a consideration of alternative ways of being and living, but most of this is retrospective and clearly triggered by our questions.

> I wish I'd, I'd come back to being intellectual there, um, perhaps I wish I'd, I, I would study more now if I was a young person, you know, I just lived to go farming, but I think now, [pause] if I had my time now I think I would sort of try and learn more and, on the science, perhaps side of it, the farming . . . I don't mean I'm envious of this granddaughter now but I mean she's doing research for Department for Environment, Food and Rural Affairs (DEFRA) and she travels . . . I mean she's only 22 or 23, she's got her degree and sort of got a very good job with DEFRA, and you

know doing some research on calves so she has to go round various farms which she had to find in the West Country and she was told she should join some research thing up in Scotland . . . And she's just had three or four days up . . . she had to sort of take her papers and explain to them all that she was doing up there. She's going off out to Spain to, something with her papers there. And I admire her and I you know, I wish perhaps I'd had the brains to do something like that . . .

(Interview 2, March 2005)

We might say that John stuck *to* his script – which is different from saying that John was stuck *in* his script. One reason for this is that to a large extent John's script 'worked' for the situations he found himself in. There was, in this regard, little reason for wanting to change his story. It fitted the particular 'ecology' of John's actions (see Biesta and Tedder 2006, 2007) – an ecology characterised by a large degree of continuity and stability. Geographically, John stayed on the same farm most of his life, moving to live a few miles away only on semi-retirement. Socially his position remained stable. Psychically he tells of no great upheavals or traumas until the end of farming in 1995. Although from the story as told it is difficult to get a feel for the economic stability, here was a farmer's son on a farm employing a number of labourers, born just before the Great Depression that affected some farmers so badly, and not a word to say about difficulty or poverty – other than a brief description of the basic living quarters on the farm. It seems likely there was a relative degree of financial security provided through the family. With nothing forcing him to move away and no desire to escape why would John need to story his life differently? He began to learn the skills of farming from age seven (though tacitly no doubt from birth), wanted to become a farmer, and became a farmer. Life happened, John could comfortably respond, shifting, tweaking, yes, but not having to expend energy on reworking. In a word John's world was farming. From his family and their employees; from auctioneers, land agents; accountants, solicitors, and other professionals; from marketing men, John was given, and later sought out farming scripts.

It was only when the ecology of John's life began to change that a discrepancy began to occur between John's script and his life. There is the whole issue of how the world changed – from gentlemanly agreement to market forces. This transformed John's world whilst he himself tried to remain constant to the original script. There is considerable evidence that John tried to operate as if the world he grew up in was still present. He idealised a world where a shake of the hand or a nod of the head indicated that a 'gentleman's agreement' had been made. Throughout much of his farming life this was substantially true. But as market forces and land agents representing his landlord entered the scene this all changed with sudden and dramatic force. John was left adrift and without a programme of action in this new world. His birthright script was redundant but he was unpractised in script development since he was primarily used to following the script he had, a script that had served him very well for most of his life.

As we have mentioned in the previous chapter, our aim is not to pass judgement on John – or for that matter on any of the other individuals we will be discussing in this book. We are interested in the stories people tell about their lives, in the things that people do in and through those stories, and in the ways in which such stories function in people's learning and action. But we are not claiming that people ought to story their life, that they ought to learn from their life, or that they should act in a particular way based on their learning. Nor are we suggesting that good or happy or fulfilled lives can only be led if they involve narration and learning. This is important to bear in mind when answering the question what can be concluded from John's case. We wish to make three observations. First of all we can see that storying was not very important or prominent in how John lived his life. We have little doubt that John, up on the hills in his Land Rover with his dog by his side, on a crisp morning with the cows all around was filled with wellbeing. It is also clear that the script that 'accompanied' John's life – his story of wanting to be a farmer and of being a farmer – served him well and offered him agentic opportunities within the particular context in which his life was lived. It is only when this context began to change that the story he had offered him little in terms of resources to engage with these changes through narrative and narration. The only thing this suggests is that the more scripted kind of narrative that we encountered in John's case offers relatively little in terms of flexibility. If, as we have suggested in the introduction, we see the life narrative as a tool, John's case thus shows both the advantages and disadvantages of having a 'strong' tool, i.e., a tool suited for particular tasks and circumstances.

3 Marie Tuck

We conducted seven interviews with Marie Tuck between December 2004 and February 2007. Much of what Marie told us about her life was presented in descriptive terms, providing a chronological overview of her life and sharing her anxieties about her children. But what is interesting is that over time the character of Marie's stories and storying began to change and became increasingly analytical and reflective. During the course of the project, so we might say, Marie began to use the stories about her life differently. This is one of the things that makes Marie's case interesting for our purposes, as it indicates how, through becoming more familiar with the 'genre' and practice of life storying, it becomes possible to do more with the 'tool' of the life narrative. As the quality of the narration changed, so did the potential to learn from and through the narration.

Marie Tuck

Marie Tuck lived in an industrial village in the south-west of England. The first interview took place in the primary school where we made contact and subsequent interviews took place in her home, a carefully maintained terraced house in the village. She was in her mid-thirties when we first met and was married to a much older man. There were two children in the family, a daughter aged six and a son aged two. Marie's husband had specialised qualifications for working in the construction industry and that meant he was often away from home when he had work and Marie carried most of the responsibility for bringing up their children.

Marie was born and grew up with her sister in a village not far from where she lived. Her father worked as an electrician and fitter for an engineering company and her mother was a nurse. She recalled being happy at school although, unlike her sister, she did not have academic aptitude and left school at the age of 16 with some Certificate in Secondary Education (CSE) qualifications. Marie had been close to her father and told stories of tomboy enthusiasms that did not incline her to study:

I'd go out and dig holes and I'd go out and like help my dad in the shed and I'd wanna be building and, and climbing the tree and making mud-pies and just doing everything like that rather than, you know, the sitting down studying and, and all this business.

(Interview 1, December 2004)

Marie's father died when she was 22. He had suffered a stroke in his mid-forties and was an invalid for the remaining nine years of his life, eventually dying from a brain haemorrhage. He left a substantial gap in her life.

Marie outlined the diversity of jobs she had after she left school. The first was a Youth Training Scheme placement with a woman who started a business making pesto. The business moved to Wales and Marie moved with the company and helped establish the factory. However, she was soon homesick and returned home. From working on a farm she concluded she was really a country girl at heart. She then spent some years working on building sites, initially as cook and tea lady for a team of road workers, but also a snagger, fixing remaining faults before a new house is handed over to its owners. She worked on the roads:

I ended up working on a road gang, with an Irish road gang? . . . [it] came up in a pub that somebody was looking for a cook, a shackler as they call it . . . weeks at a time in digs and all this business looking after these, anywhere from seven to fourteen blokes making sure they had breakfast, dinner and tea, and the abuse that went with it, but I [laughs] which I – it's the sort of thing I enjoy really . . . I used to go out on the roads and help them do work out on the roads as well. This is where I met my husband while I was in the ditch. I was in a ditch with a whacker at the time.

(Interview 1, December 2004)

Marie's husband lived in London and used to visit the south-west as part of what she called a 'motorcycle club'. He was 17 years older than Marie, had been involved in other relationships and was the father of two daughters only a few years younger than Marie herself. For a time Marie moved to London and worked collecting money from pub fruit machines. The couple spent several years leading an active social life centred on motorbikes and the pub, but at the age of 29, Marie fell pregnant. She and her husband decided on a change of direction: they married soon after the baby was born, they arranged a mortgage to buy a house and settled for a more conventional way of life. Their first child was a daughter and a son was born four years later.

Marie reflected on this key transition that:

He was already winding down a bit really. The club had disbanded and it was sort of a strange transition really because it was almost like mourning. You know, it was something that he'd done for 30 years and something that I'd done for a good ten, and, and it was strange. All of a sudden we didn't have that anymore.

(Interview 1, December 2004)

She could not recall a definite point at which a decision was made and said they had been having fun for years but such a lifestyle was not very stable:

Somewhere, I'm not quite sure at what point we came out of it, [we] decided we didn't want to be doing so much of that any more ... now my husband's into fishing instead of motorbikes. [laughs] So it's quite a little bit of a life-change really, you know, from, from living in the pub basically to, you know, wanting the best for our children and looking after our house.

(Interview 1, December 2004)

In the interviews we conducted in 2005, Marie was committed to making her family life a success. The stories she told us focused particularly on her life as home-maker and mother. She told us of contacts with her daughter's primary school and of how she was dealing with their expectations of parental support for children's learning. She attended a part-time literacy course for a year to find out more about supporting her children. Marie became engaged actively with life in the village, supporting the primary school in their gardening and recycling projects and serving as Chair of the local playgroup committee.

Marie told us also about some of the behavioural problems she was experiencing with her daughter and how it reminded her of her own rebelliousness as a child. For Marie the challenges of being a parent seem to have triggered a re-examination and re-evaluation of her own youthful behaviour. She spoke of the limits of her personal control over her daughter:

I know my parents brought me up with good values, good moral values ... to go through life but it didn't stop me being particularly naughty for a while but, I suppose this is why I want to instil it in my daughter's head so that she will behave herself. She's not going out and, you know, running riot with me.

(Interview 1, December 2004)

Marie felt some remorse about the way she behaved with her own mother – 'I'd have liked not to have put my mother through hell.' She thought it possible to learn from that experience although, when asked to specify what she might have learned, her response suggested that there are some things in life which are just inevitable:

> I've learned that it's not nice to be not nice to your parents, I suppose, but then you can't explain that to a child, can you? They're not going to see that until they're my age, and then they'll start apologising like I am to my mother . . . But I can hear [my daughter] saying things that I used to say, 'No, I'm not doing that, I'm not doing it and that's that,' and I used to do that to my mother.
>
> (Interview 1, December 2004)

Marie was also experiencing problems with her son. She told us in several interviews of her anxieties about his speech development and told us of the ways she was engaging with different people in efforts to secure a reliable diagnosis and treatment of his problems.

> So I just want it [to] come through sooner rather than later, because it's just, it just feels like limboing [at] the moment, you know. I want, I want, I want somebody to see my son and sort him out. Now!
>
> (Interview 2, May 2005)

She wanted someone in authority to take action. Through the health visitor and through her doctor she was trying to get further diagnosis and testing sooner than was routine, which would normally mean a wait of up to five months. Marie was frustrated by her inability to secure action about a potential disability and her frustration was exacerbated by a change in the practice of health visitors. She said that no longer could she expect scheduled visits to ensure the welfare of her child; instead it would be her own responsibility to contact health visitors if she were experiencing problems.

When she talked about her voluntary and income-earning activities outside the home, it became evident that Marie had learned many skills and talents from her earlier working life. At home and through the school, she was learning new skills in gardening, composting and recycling. Marie said she really would like a recycling job. It emerged that Marie had a Public Service Vehicle (PSV) driver's licence when she told how she had been 'head-hunted' to do a school run for a local bus company.

However, Marie seemed not to value her versatility and instead commented on her regrets at not finding a single vocation that was right for her:

> [M]y mum always says, 'One day you'll find your vocation,' you know, or 'Yes, you're very good at everything that you try and do,' you know, 'I'd, I'd

love it if you could find your vocation in life, you know? Your, the thing that you love doing and are good at.' . . . I just think there's got to be a job out there for me somewhere.

(Interview 2, May 2005)

Marie spoke of the effect of her husband working so regularly away from home and told a story of meeting another woman in the village who had the impression she was a single parent, an impression she was keen to dispel:

> I was down at the club . . . talking to somebody that I've only ever really said 'hello' to . . . I've lived here six years, been married most of that time while I've been here, and as you know, been with my partner 13 years and she thought I was a single mother . . . not that there's anything wrong with being a single mother, but I, you know, I'm pretty chuffed that I'm not and um I dunno it makes me wonder what people think.

(Interview 4, November 2005)

In our interviews in 2006 it became evident that the family had financial diffi-culties. In part the difficulties arose because Marie's husband had work prob-lems: he could not afford to update his qualifications which meant the construction jobs he could do were boring and poorly paid:

> [E]very time they run out you've got to redo them at full whack and, you know, a week off work to do it and it's just, money making, it really is you know . . . basically you got to pay to work haven't you? . . . Well he ain't got an awful lot left at the minute because we haven't been able to afford to replace them all. His ADR, which is a diesel carrying ticket, like a diesel bowser, you know, they go around and fill up all the big machines that are out there . . . there's so much more to think about . . . whereas at the moment, he's just going from A to B with a load, a load of muck. Basically which is, you know, it is they call it a dead-man's job. It's boring, very, very boring.

(Interview 5, June 2006)

With the complications of making suitable childcare arrangements, Marie said she had been unable to continue her bus-driving job for more than a few months. However, she had an ambition to drive lorries and she seemed deter-mined eventually to achieve this aspiration:

Somebody said to me, 'Oh, no haulage company's going to employ you for like those hours of a day, you know. If you can't do a full ten-hour shift,' and I'm like, 'Well, we'll see, you know, we'll see, we'll see. Where there's a will there's a way.' 'Create a job and convince somebody that they want you to do it,' is what I say. [laughs] I'm working on this theory at the moment, but um it's not working so far.

(Interview 5, June 2006)

In the meantime, Marie watched out for opportunities for part-time work to supplement the family income. She earned money by cleaning and ironing for friends in the village and repeatedly stated her intention to find more paid employment when her son was older. She had become more involved in recycling, outlining what she had learned about being a 'skip rat' – someone who goes to the recycling centre with a boot load of stuff and comes back with even more; or about being a 'dump buddy' – someone who'll help you with repairs to the things you want to recycle. Eventually Marie's interest in recycling led to her securing a congenial part-time job in a local authority recycling centre.

As the financial problems grew, so it became increasingly evident that Marie's relationship with her husband was becoming strained. He was living in the family home and had periods of short-term employment and self-employment in the local area but Marie was frustrated by his ineffectiveness at keeping a job and his unreliability in supporting family life. It appeared during the fifth and sixth interviews that she wanted their relationship to survive but felt undermined by a lack of reciprocity and co-operation. She was annoyed that he needed to be asked repeatedly to do things:

I find that . . . that makes me feel un-regarded, un-appreciated . . . Whereas all my thoughts are about my family and what their needs and wants are and I just don't think it's too much to ask to expect the same thing back. I appreciate men don't necessarily think that way, but you know, I think after 15 years that he might have a little bit of a clue about how I tick.

(Interview 6, September 2006)

The difficulties of the situation were exacerbated by the fact that Marie broke her foot and was incapacitated at the time our penultimate interview took place:

I don't think I've stopped crying for a fortnight, 'scuse me [in tears], but it is, it is so frustrating. You know, my car is parked up out there, I can't get anywhere, I can't see anybody . . . It's been hard the last couple of weeks . . .

he's still gone off – went fishing for the weekend and I'm here with the kids for the weekend and yeah, I deal with it, I cope with it, I want him to have his respite, I want him to have his, you know, his hobby . . . I just don't feel that it's reciprocated.

(Interview 6, September 2006)

Marie's efforts to forge a conventional lifestyle with husband, children and a home were not succeeding. Her account of the situation indicated that her husband was unable to provide the regular income and stability that would sustain their way of life and was ineffective at supporting Marie's own efforts to make up the deficit with her various part-time jobs. What was becoming increasingly attractive to her was an alternative and independent future: without the burden of her husband Marie could still care for her children and enjoy again some of the freedoms and friendships that she had enjoyed before her marriage. Our sixth interview recorded how this was becoming a distinct possibility.

In the seventh and final interview Marie described how she had started a relationship with someone else a year earlier with the explicit purpose of ending her marriage and regaining her independence. Of her relationship with her husband she said:

I was dying, I was dying . . . I really felt like it was killing me softly you know . . . my mum said to me the other day, . . . she said, 'You were shaking and you said, "Mum, he's sucking the life out of me".' And that's how I felt, I felt like I was waning away.

(Interview 7, February 2007)

She had no intention of continuing the new relationship she had started:

[H]e was a means to an end and you know . . . I wouldn't go from frying pan to fire . . . and I'm like, 'Right, listen, been there, done that, right. I'm an independent single mother of two that can stand on her own two feet, doesn't need you or anybody else. Don't want you or anybody else.' . . . And I just felt so bloody good, I tell ya, and I still do.

(Interview 7, February 2007)

There was a degree of pride but also pathos and humour in her story of the break-up:

I'm dead chuffed with meself to have done this. Do you know when I did it? New Year's Eve . . . 'cause at twelve o'clock I don't, I don't wanna hug and kiss anybody, let alone [my husband] and say you know, 'Happy New Year'. Because that wasn't, that wasn't happening. So [we] sat here in separate rooms, I had a bowl of onion soup, watching the fireworks on the telly and he come in and quite, it was quite weird because he didn't know which way anything was going to go, you know? He just came in and let a party-popper off in me soup.

(Interview 7, February 2007)

When we last spoke with Marie, some months after the final interview, the house had been sold and Marie was moving with her children to rented accommodation in another village. Her husband had started divorce proceedings but the process was not a smooth one.

Narrative quality

One of the interesting features of our interviews with Marie Tuck is that, while the stories she told in earlier interviews were predominantly descriptive, in later interviews the stories became more reflective and evaluative. The narrative quality of Marie's stories thus changed significantly over time. In later interviews she revisited events in her life and deepened her account – and understanding – of them, focusing more on themes and issues that were troubling her and on the actions she had taken or was planning to take to make changes in her life. It could be that Marie had become more comfortable with the interview process and with the opportunities it provided for her to talk about and reflect upon her life. It certainly seemed serendipitous that the project interviews happened to coincide with a time when she needed to reflect on a major transition in her life.

After some apprehension about the first interview Marie proved to be a keen participant in the project and spoke openly and at length during interviews. Marie's stories were told from a first person perspective and were usually about her experiences, decisions, achievements and disappointments. Her stories tended to have an unrehearsed and spontaneous quality; they did not convey a sense of having been practised either internally or with others. She did not use the technique of recreating dialogues that some respondents used in their stories.

The shift in the narrative quality of her stories was apparent in the way a plot began to emerge, a plot that had to do with Marie's wish to be independent and in control of her life. This increasingly became the basic theme and organising principle of Marie's narrative. The shift was most noticeably visible in her relationship with her husband but was also evident in her nostalgia for the biker lifestyle she used to lead. The plot not only provides structure and coherence in her life story but also appears as a driving force in the way in which she accounted for her life and gave direction to it. Learning, identity and agency thus seemed to come together in Marie's life narrative.

Marie's stories displayed a high element of justification. In talking about her life she clearly tried to make plausible why she had done everything in her life the way she had, constantly showing that what may seem odd from the outside – her work with the road gang, her life as a biker – actually fitted in very well with the way she wanted to lead her life. In one observation about the deteriorating relationship with her husband, she explained that he was making a life transition earlier than she was, and that served as a justification for the action she planned to take:

> he's sort of made another little transitional thing I feel now, whereas he's moved on a bit, and moved on to his boats, and he's doing all that thing, where I – it suddenly dawned on me, now the kids are getting a bit older, that I haven't finished doing what I was doing before the kids . . . I'm not ready to stop that, you know. I've calmed down a bit. I've had me kids, you know, I've got a sense of priority, you know, I know what comes first, but after that, you know, still, I still, I still wanna have a bit of fun, you know, and still enjoy doing the things that I did before.
>
> (Interview 5, June 2006)

There was little analysis in Marie's stories using frameworks that might be termed academic – there was little elaboration of her stories, for example, by using political or historical contexts. Nevertheless, her aspiration to have control of her life seemed to have an idealistic, even ideological quality. Marie's stories reveal her to have been rebellious against gender and class norms in her youth. She saw herself continuing this quality even within the context of being a mother:

> society expects you to – you know, I'm a mother and, you know, so I'm a little bit of a mad mother sometimes, you know, so, so what? you know? Nothing bad, nothing, you know, I'm still a person, that's what I think has been bothering me a bit lately, and I suppose in a sense when you're told not to do something, you want to do it even more don't ya, and when someone's expecting you to do something you don't wanna disappoint them [laughs].
>
> (Interview 5, June 2006)

Efficacy: Learning potential and action potential

When we ask what kind of opportunities for learning and action Marie's narratives provided, it is clear that she found the interviews useful as they provided her with opportunities to 'externalise' her experiences, feelings and insights about her life. Her overall view about taking part in the project was that she found it encouraging to think about her life and self – 'questioning myself' as she put it – although she could not articulate any particular respects in which it had been helpful:

> Interesting, to be honest. Yea, 'cause it does give you food for thought and it is, you know, in a way quite probing but self-probing . . . I have been questioning an awful lot of things in my life, for a long time. I probably, I suppose, [pause] the, the period of time that I've known you, is probably been the most . . . And I don't know if it sort of helped, don't know. But yea, no, I have been . . . questioning myself and everything about everything for a long time.
>
> (Interview 7, February 2007)

The interviews were not the only opportunity she had for this. In the last interview she mentioned that she had a group of women friends – some with daughters of a similar age to Marie's – that she met regularly:

> M . . . and I were sitting until quite late last night here, sort of analysing a few things and chewing the fat you know, and putting the world to rights 'cause it helps, it does help . . . I feel so different to, to people, other people I know that are, nothing like me or, or M . . . or my friend K . . ., um, but what *is* that, that makes us different? And *why*, you know?
>
> (Interview 7, February 2007)

The opportunities to learn from and through the narration shifted over time and coincided with the shift in narrative quality. When the narration becomes more analytical and reflective opportunities to learn from narrative and narration begin to emerge. During the first four interviews, Marie's stories recount her experiences as an active wife, mother and home-maker, someone who would undertake casual paid work to supplement family income and work as a volunteer in her community. From the fifth interview, however, her stories articulate strongly what she has learned from her life, particularly about herself and her relationships with others. She has learned that she is a person who wants to be independent and free of male constraints. She has also learned what independence means and what its price is. There are elements of pride and of sadness in the way in which she talks about how she manages to regain some of her independence. This is the plot that increasingly begins to emerge as an organising principle in Marie's stories and also, we suggest, in Marie's life.

Whereas Marie's narrative remains on the descriptive side of the spectrum compared to some of the other participants in the project whose stories are much more probing and much more aimed at generating ways to understand their lives, the most significant difference between John Peel and Marie lies in the fact that Marie's narrative is 'under construction'. There is no fixed 'script' to which Marie adheres in her storying, but a constant *contemporaneous* set of articulations and reflections. The main difference between John Peel's and Marie Tuck's narrative, so we might say, lies in its flexibility rather than in its analytical depth. This appears to give Marie's narrative a greater efficacy in dealing with changing situations. Because it is contemporaneous and flexible, Marie's storying not only figures as a 'site' of reflection and learning, but as a 'site' of reflection and learning that clearly has an impact on her action and agency.

We would not claim that asking Marie questions about her life led to her growing dissatisfaction but it appears that the kinds of questions we asked in our interviews were consonant with the questions she was asking herself about her life. Her most agentic undertaking was effecting the transition to being a single mother. She rejects her husband's negative outlook on life and the hard work it causes her in favour of a new life:

> I just can't cope with the misery and . . . I don't know, everything was neg-
> ative and I just, that's just, I just can't. And I, I couldn't pull him out of it
> . . . I intend to sort of start living again without feeling guilty [laughs]. And
> I just can't wait, I'm just so looking forward to the rest of it, you know? . . .
> I just woke up and I thought, 'No, god, no I can't do this. I can't imagine
> doing this for another however long. I don't want to be this miserable, life
> doesn't have to . . .' I'm a happy person, generally, you know. And I just, I
> was in danger of going, going down with him.
>
> (Interview 7, February 2007)

Of her new life she said:

> It, it was, it was really strange and I sort of analysed it to myself . . . I've
> been in a funny place and I'm not quite sure where that is, but I'm not there
> anymore . . . I've got what I wanted which is, that's it, it's finished, done . . .
> what happens from here on in is, is . . . I, I'll make it happen and it's not
> down to anybody else.
>
> (Interview 7, February 2007)

For Marie storying increasingly became a useful 'tool' for reflection and action and it was the flexible and contemporaneous character of the tool – i.e., the fact that her storying was evolving rather than fixed, that it was closely connected to what was happening in her life, and that it was increasingly being organised around a particular plot – that allowed Marie to learn from her storying and to translate this learning into action.

4   Maggie Holman

Maggie Holman had a capacity to tell detailed, complex, sophisticated and elaborate stories about her life. In this regard her stories differ from those of John Peel and Marie Tuck. But although Maggie's narration can be characterised as elaborate and in this regard has a high narrative intensity, there is little analysis and reflection in her stories, even though there is judgement. Maggie's case thus raises important questions about the conditions under which learning from more detailed narratives can take place. Maggie was also one of the few participants who used a thematic rather than a chronological way to talk about her life. It is the absence of chronology and sequentiality in Maggie's stories that raises important questions about the way in which narrative learning operates.

Maggie Holman

Maggie Holman could be regarded as a bohemian who has learned domesticity: her story is one of learning to reconcile her creative impulses as an artist and singer with the demands of everyday living with a husband and two young sons. Maggie has always been interested in art and music. She studied for a degree in fine art and earned her living for more than a decade from commercial graphic work. She continues to undertake creative craft work and photography but has decided that her main responsibilities are for organising a supportive home for her musically accomplished husband and children.

Seven interviews lasting between one-and-a-half hours and two hours took place with Maggie between November 2004 and January 2007. The interviews all took place in the family home, a Victorian semi-detached house that was clean, tidy and well-kept with a small garden. In the room where we met the furniture and household goods were functional and inexpensive; there were bookshelves with a few novels and a substantial number of reference books; there was a television set with a small screen and a video recorder. Maggie's artistic sensibility was apparent in the quality of the pictures on the walls, including some fine watercolours. The original works included pieces by her father as well as by herself. The fact that their house was her husband's work-place – he teaches the piano – was evident during our interviews when a prac-tising musician could sometimes be heard.

Maggie proved to be an articulate woman who appeared very engaged with the project and keen to talk about her life for at least the first three interviews. However, she started to express reservations about the purpose of the inter-views and, by the seventh, seemed relieved that they were ending. She said it was not an experience she would want to repeat:

> I wouldn't want to do it again um because I'd feel I've done it, and it's, in some way it's been like tidying up and putting it all into order and putting it away, and I suppose that's been very useful. Um, I don't *need* to do it anymore.
>
> (Interview 7, January 2007)

When we first interviewed her in November 2004, Maggie was aged 49. She was born in a remote part of the south-west of England where her father's family worked in farming and banking. Maggie depicted her father as someone with artistic aspirations who tried a variety of jobs before finding his métier as a self-employed picture framer, which suited his 'precise' and 'meticulous' approach to work. He met Maggie's mother, a primary school teacher who 'was known to be one of the old fashioned strict sort and the children were fright-ened of her' (Interview 1, November 2004). They had two children – Maggie and her brother.

Maggie's earliest memories were of her fascination with colour:

> the very first time I fell over and cut my knee as a toddler and howled and screamed as children do and then I looked down and there was this bright red splodge and I sort of stopped crying and had gone completely silent and said 'Oh what a lovely colour' and [my mother] dabbed me with a handkerchief and it had all gone bright red and I *begged* to be allowed to keep this handkerchief.
>
> (Interview 2, March 2005)

Maggie attended the school where her mother taught but, with her artistic inclinations, she always felt out of place. She found she was a middle-class girl speaking with a middle-class accent in a school with a predominantly rural working-class catchment and she said she was picked on and teased even though she had been born and belonged there as much as the other children. However, Maggie commented of herself at junior school that:

I was just utterly stuck-up . . . I couldn't make friends with children who didn't even know their alphabet! They played in the sand pit and they used to bomb me with sand and I was frightened of them . . . And I hid in a corner and . . . and just did drawing and colouring when they were all running around.

> (Interview 1, November 2004)

Maggie passed the eleven plus examination, which she attributed to her ability to excel with mathematical tests, and secured an assisted place at a convent school. Her mother was pleased because she thought the girls were politer there than girls at other secondary schools. Maggie was dismissive of the convent experience:

Our school engendered no aspirations whatsoever other than becoming a nurse or a teacher because it was an all girls school and girls don't do things like have careers or do anything very academic.

> (Interview 1, November 2004)

She said the nuns did little to foster her artistic and musical potential; the school had 'a very dead outlook on some things' (Interview 3, April 2005). She continued to be rather solitary at school: 'all the rest of my class were into horses and I was the only person who wasn't and I didn't have any friends as a result' (Interview 3, April 2005). Nevertheless, she left with GCE qualifications that enabled her to undertake a foundation course at the art school in her home town that she found:

absolutely superb and it was a breath of fresh air after seven years at this rather stultifying school . . . I was never happier than the first six months of that year.

> (Interview 1, November 2004)

The foundation course was followed by four years at an art college about 100 miles from home. We discussed what had contributed to the decision to move away from home and undertake a fine art degree and Maggie suggested that the choice of an art career was not fully hers. She could recall few logical reasons for the decision to go to art school: she first saw the school on a sunny day; she disliked the poster from a competing art school. What was more at issue was the *kind* of art course she would enrol for:

I was going to have a career; nobody considered what sort of a career. My father had a great expectation that I'd do something with art, because . . .

he had a lot of unfulfilled dreams of his own and had been prevented from going to art school, because his family had believed that art was an unreliable and effeminate thing to do and ... [he] wanted me to go and do all the things that he had never been allowed to do ... I think the big question was not 'what will she do with her life?' but, 'what sort of art will she do? Will it be art history, will it be museum restoration, picture framing, commercial art, fine art, what?' But it had to be art.

(Interview 4, October 2005)

The advice from her tutors at the local art school was that she should only take fine art if she were convinced it was right for her because it would not provide training for a career. Years later she judged this 'very sound advice indeed' but the advice of a family friend appeared to carry more weight at the time:

this other friend of dad's, ..., um said, 'Stuff and nonsense! You should, if you want to do fine art, do fine art,' and I immediately glamorised myself as somebody who needs, needs to be a painter and um, did this sort of Victorian melodrama thing and decided that that's what I would do ... so that was my solution to life was um to invent an ivory tower, a glamorous princess role for myself.

(Interview 5, May 2006)

In retrospect, Maggie says she would have liked to undertake a graphics course. At that time, however, she didn't know what she didn't know and was in no position to choose such an option:

I didn't know when I went off to art school initially that I'd be quite so interested in typefaces and lettering and I had no idea that that would be an absorbing passion and that I might have had a career in graphics – and if that had happened then all of this might have been different.

(Interview 4, October 2005)

So Maggie studied for a fine art degree which she described as 'a very artificial and strange environment' (Interview 1, November 2004). She seemed almost to regret that 'we were given a full grant to sort of bum around for four years really and be creative and ... I was far too immature to make best use of that' (Interview 1, November 2004). She appreciated the space and ambience she was given in which to paint but had reservations about the teaching and the curriculum:

But the whole system was terribly open-ended and lazy and vague and ... there was a notable *lack* of technical teaching. Always this 'you have to find your own voice and that means you find your own way of handling a paint-brush as well.'

(Interview 2, March 2005)

We discussed Maggie's learning outwith her degree studies and how she coped with being a student in the 1970s. She felt ill-prepared for independent life: 'Life skills! I was just *nowhere*, I had *no* idea' (Interview 2, March 2005). She spoke of living in a college hostel which, in those days, was supposed to be seg-regated with separate entrances and separate accommodation for men and women. Maggie reflected on the challenge of being a girl with a convent edu-cation in the environment of a 1970s art school:

> I did some extremely stupid things in the course of those few years and my mother had no idea of the half of it . . . I resented the fact that parents seemed to have absolutely different sets of rules for their sons than for their daughters.

(Interview 2, March 2005)

After the first year Maggie felt she settled down, found some conducive digs and started to paint pictures of rooftops, chimneys and back lanes in the area of town where she lived. It appeared to be a period of transition in which Maggie gained the knowledge, skills and attitudes she needed to function as an artist and as an adult:

> I was there for four years, and I spent . . . the first year, absolutely floun-dering about and not knowing what to do and I suppose it wasn't a waste of time in that you need to sort out these thoughts and find your direction . . . I had to catch up with a lot of childhood that I hadn't done and grow up socially and grow up mentally in all sorts of ways, as well as trying to decide what sort of an artist I was.

(Interview 3, April 2005)

While attending the art school, Maggie found employment with a stationer in the local town. What started as a Saturday job eventually became full-time, with Maggie selling art materials to local people. Later she worked for the same company as a self-employed graphic artist for several years. She undertook drawings for brochures of hotels and guest-houses. She taught herself callig-raphy to undertake commercial work like menus for restaurants and cafes. In the days before computers, Maggie learned to 'cut and paste' with real paper, cow gum, pencils and set-squares. She would physically fit type around a pho-tograph when producing booklets for local firms. She became familiar with typefaces from selling Letraset. She learned from her employer the basic business skills of setting out an invoice and dealing with non-paying customers. Maggie had to develop her skills as a graphic artist and as a business person from scratch, she had no prior training in these fields; however, the fact that she was still learning and lacked formal qualifications constrained her ability to charge for her work:

> I found the commercial aspects of the business side of it very, *very* difficult and I hated charging for what I did . . . I felt very undermined by not having done, not having any professional qualifications because I'd done a fine art course and fundamentally I felt a fraud.
>
> (Interview 3, April 2005)

Maggie became increasingly involved in choral singing when she worked as a graphic artist and eventually met her husband through her choir. Both were in their thirties by the time they married and they subsequently became the parents of two boys. Maggie's life underwent a transition to a new period that revolves around her husband, his work at home as a music teacher, their sons and their education.

At home, Maggie had settled into using her graphics abilities not for commercial use, but for designing posters and programmes for choir concerts. She continued to be an active member of a local choir and said that her social life revolved around the choir. She used her artistic talents domestically, for crocheting blankets and making curtains. She made a brief foray into commercial painting by producing a style of work as a commercial venture but the market for this work did not endure. At our first interview, there were regrets in Maggie's account that she did not have a social context that would enable her to use her fine art abilities:

> I will never be a painter because I've . . . got a life that's crowded out with people and commitments and children to collect from school and pupils coming here and the noise of the piano and everything going on.
>
> (Interview 1, November 2004)

There were also physical limitations – Maggie said she no longer had the ability to undertake the intricately detailed paintings that she created when she was a student (and of which there are examples in her house). Apart from which, she thought it would be extremely difficult to have sufficient uninterrupted time to allow her to undertake such work.

Maggie had little aspiration to return to a life as a graphic artist but nevertheless had aspirations to have a job.

> I have times when I *hate* feeling that I'm *just* a housewife and a dogsbody
> . . . and most women in my position go out to work . . . A corner of me
> would love to have a part-time job, possibly . . . doing graphic design on a
> computer in some, working for a printer, I'd love to do that.
>
> (Interview 3, April 2005)

Much of Maggie's time was taken up with family responsibilities: supporting
her husband and organising the children. In the period covered by our project,
the death of Maggie's father occurred as well as the death of an uncle, so perhaps she was more than usually aware of family matters. She also had responsibility for the care of her elderly and increasingly frail mother-in-law. She
commented on the changes she has seen:

> it's strange to see somebody who's always been demanding and difficult
> and stubborn and obstinate and thoroughly [sighs] demanding on your
> patience and time in every way, suddenly so meek, that you really fear that
> this maybe um, I would almost rather have her fighting spirit back.
>
> (Interview 5, May 2006)

She managed to find the resources to cope:

> you just get on do all of it because you have to because there is no choice
> and it's there and it's yours and you don't think twice. Once the situation is
> in front of you, you do it and I suppose you learn that you have skills you
> didn't know you had and resources you didn't know you had.
>
> (Interview 5, May 2006)

The learning that had interested Maggie in recent times had been the achievement of proficiency in using a computer. She attended her first computer
course to learn about Microsoft Publisher, shortly before acquiring her first
computer in May 2000. She had since acquired an Apple Mac. Her learning
over the intervening years included some formal sessions: undertaking a
beginner's course – Computer Literacy and Information Technology (CLAIT)
– to learn basic programs like Word, Excel and Access and also a course to
learn to use QUARK, the industry standard professional design program.
Informally at home, with her Apple Mac, she has learned to use Adobe
InDesign and other graphics programs.

Maggie identified a wide range of domestic uses for her computer: Internet
banking; emails for herself and her husband; scanning photographs; finding
and downloading fonts; designing concert programmes for her own choir and
for others; using a search engine and key words for research purposes; keeping

records of her husband's business accounts and exam results. Her sons used the computer for musical composition and for learning music theory as well as for more ordinary homework, for researching and writing projects for different school subjects. Maggie admitted to spending a great deal of time working with her computer and commented wryly:

> You're learning how to solve a problem which, if you didn't have the computer, you wouldn't need to solve!
>
> (Interview 3, April 2005)

She described with particular enthusiasm how her interest in digital photography had developed, that she had bought a digital SLR camera and was taking hundreds of photos. In some respects, this had become a substitute for painting: the results are instant and can be viewed and processed on a computer. Sometimes, however, the images she photographs make her want to paint again. Rather wistfully she concluded:

> the [school] drive is just beautiful and if you're driving and it's raining and you've got the wet car windscreen this watery impressionistic wash of green and coloured flowers um it's really quite lovely and um I've been *desperate* to do something about this other than just take photographs and yesterday I did get up to the attic and try to start painting again for the first time for a long time. But it won't go very far, I'm sure.
>
> (Interview 5, May 2006)

Narrative quality

Maggie is an articulate and well-educated woman who was capable of making a variety of responses to interview questions and a simple characterisation of her stories is not straightforward. Her stories were descriptive of personal experiences when she gave an account of such events as holiday outings, or when describing activities she shared with her husband or her sons, and her accounts of such experiences were richly detailed. Our interviews invited her to be reflective on her earlier life and learning and in response she was frequently highly critical of her young self as snobbish and 'stuck up', as absurd or stupid. She was inclined to make negative judgments about institutions such as her convent school and the college that she attended for her fine art degree. A tendency to self-deprecation continued in her stories about her current life that she was inclined to characterise as boring and uneventful, and she remarked frequently on what she saw as her inadequacies and failings. Thus Maggie tended to be judgemental in the stories she told about her life.

However, there seemed to be little empathy with the people she talked about, little concern to understand her younger self or other people. Maggie's stories were not told so that reflection might lead to empathy and understanding. In this regard we might say that whereas at one level her stories were characterised by a relatively high degree of narrative intensity – length, detail, complexity of the accounts offered – they were descriptive and judgemental but not explicitly reflective. It was difficult, in other words, to get a sense of any learning that was occurring in and through the stories Maggie told about her life.

Maggie came closer than many of our participants to adopting a 'thematic' rather than 'chronological' approach to retelling her life story by starting with an assertion that she had always been interested in 'colour'. The very first point Maggie made in her first interview was about the importance to her of colour:

> I always wanted to do something with colours . . . as a child I used to play with coloured clothes pegs on the floor . . . and go into an art shop or a stationery shop I would just drool over rows and rows of paints and coloured felt tipped pens and rows, pieces of coloured tissue paper . . . I have to have that.
>
> (Interview 1, November 2004)

The notion of becoming an artist featured as a central theme throughout Maggie's stories of her formal education, through school and into art college and to the achievement of her fine art degree. However, in retrospect she regretted the lack of specific training that could be used to enable her to earn a living. The knowledge and skills needed for calligraphy and business were self-taught when she became a self-employed graphic artist and had not featured in her formal training. Although the artist identity was an important theme in the way in which Maggie told her story, the plot that organised her narrative had more to do with a key turning point in her life when she stopped trying to live as a graphic artist and started on the phase when she would become a wife and mother. We learned more in later interviews about the nature of this transition: how Maggie had given up a long-term relationship and had started a primary teacher education course in order to effect change. One of the consequences of starting teacher education was that it necessitated having a base in a new place. In the event, marriage became possible with a man she met through her choir, an encounter that was closer to home than she anticipated. Thus the plot appears to be one of an artist becoming a wife and mother. Maggie recognised this plot in the way she judged her life as a graphic artist as being directionless while becoming married gave her life new purpose.

One interesting aspect of Maggie's narratives was her ability to bring to her stories bodies of knowledge to make them (more) meaningful. In this regard we might say that to some extent her narratives were *theorised*. It would be fair to call this approach a justificatory one because she was repeatedly self-critical about her younger self and about her current inadequacies and the stories served to provide some thread of explanation for her perceived limitations. In the comments that follow, we consider the insights from her stories given by three framing sets of knowledge. The first was that she was more familiar than many respondents with the stories of earlier generations of her family and used such knowledge to trace formative elements in her own life. The second was that she was able to use her artistic knowledge and sensibility to reflect on her life. The third significant field of knowledge came from her reading popular psychology about phenomena such as Asperger's Syndrome and this provided a tool for self-analysis.

Maggie was knowledgeable about the lives of her parents and grandparents, where they came from, what were the key events in their lives and she used this knowledge in her stories. The family she portrayed was characterful, even eccentric. Her maternal grandmother, for example, had come from Wales where she had been one of eleven sisters, three of whom married clergymen. Maggie's grandmother became the wife of a rector who died in 1925 leaving a widow and two small children who had to leave their spacious rectory and move to a smaller house in a town some miles away. It seemed the children were very proprietorial of local amenities:

> because [their house] bordered on the park they assumed that the park was theirs . . . So each of them stood sentry at the two park gates, mum at one gate and her brother at the other gate stopping any other children coming in . . . they behaved outrageously and they were two very spoiled children I think, and ultimately they were packed off to boarding school.
> (Interview 2, March 2005)

Maggie's mother was born in 1919 and died in 1990 and she observed that 'the women leave it terribly late to have their children so all of our grandparents are *old* when we're small children'. She thought of her mother as 'a child of a bygone age' and this helped her to explain why she did not access the popular culture of her youth in the 1960s and 1970s. Maggie herself thought such knowledge was necessary for survival: 'You have to have some street cred' (Interview 2, March 2005). In this way, Maggie used stories to explain her mother's 'snobbish' outlook and as a way of understanding the quality of her own childhood.

In talking about her artistic development, Maggie gave an account of what she learned from one inspirational teacher in her home town when she was undertaking her foundation degree:

She did oil painting in her own home . . . She lived in a very modern house with a central courtyard. It was a house built in a square with a hole in the middle . . . it's a very sort of, steel tube and plastic and clean and modern . . . She did big canvasses which were divided into squares and were grids of colour that she said were based on the sky . . . and she was fascinated by white with just the minutest bit of very, very pale green next to a white with a very, very, pale pink and they were all very, clean-edged, hard-edged squares and that's what her canvasses were . . . But she made me look at white . . . colour had always been for me something very bright and positive and child-like and suddenly colour was sort of a very subtle, interesting thing.

(Interview 1, November 2004)

Such a story suggests that Maggie learns from experience, but her learning is by engagement, by looking, rather than by (cognitive) reflection on the experience.

With respect to her understanding of Asperger's Syndrome, Maggie said that she had read *The Curious Incident of the Dog in the Night-time* shortly before the first interview. She thought herself 'probably a very strange person' as a child and, in the light of her reading, thought she could recognise Asperger's Syndrome, 'all sorts of self-centred attitudes and inabilities to see things from other people's point of view' (Interview 1, November 2004). She returned to this theme in a later interview as a means of interpreting her early life: she recalled rather obsessive behaviour, that she was self-centred and lacking in social skills, that she had creative interests, a talent for mathematics and synaesthesia. These 'symptoms' have become incorporated within an understanding of herself as someone who has overcome a 'mild' affliction with Asperger's. She has learned ways of dealing with her unusual qualities so they no longer create a problem:

I was very mild and I've overcome a lot of it . . . You have to learn to behave in a way that you gradually realise people expect you to behave and you have to learn to make eye contact . . . I remember being very, knowing that I was being very gauche and very awkward socially as a teenager. I know, I remember having to learn to do social things that other people find come naturally.

(Interview 6, September 2006)

Efficacy: Learning potential and action potential

When we ask what kind of opportunities for learning and action Maggie's narrative and narration provided, there is evidence that she felt that relatively little can be learned through narrative and narration. This, at least, became clear from the way in which she engaged with and commented upon the interviews. Maggie initially enjoyed the interviews and took a close interest in the transcripts. She read the transcript of the first interview before the second and suggested amendments to the text, subsequently emailing a corrected version. She even said she would be interested in reviewing a recording of the interview. However, when asked for her feelings about taking part in the project in the final interview, Maggie was discontented because she thought she had not prepared for interviews in the way she should and had not kept a diary as she said she would. The novelty had worn off. With regard to the transcripts, Maggie hated the syntactical errors, mis-spellings, and the appearance of some vocabulary that she did not think she would have used, the lack of coherence. She found them unbelievably long.

> As it's gone on it's become slightly less of a novelty. [Laughs] I think sometimes I'm [pause] probably wondering where it's going, hoping it's useful to you, and thinking well can it be, especially this um – my not really having been able to focus on how I learn, or actually learning anything anyway.
>
> (Interview 7, January 2007)

Her response suggests that Maggie did not believe she learns through processes of narration or by reading her stories. Our transcripts suggest that, in revisiting certain stories from her life, the insights she achieved (or that she chose to share) became deeper. However, Maggie herself seemed not to see her stories in this way and instead found they confirm how 'waffley' her life is:

> I haven't actually been on any particular courses in any formal way. . . . If I had it would have probably been very useful to record, um [pause] week by week, stuff from the college. I mean if you're not doing, undergoing any formal learning, um it all becomes very waffley, and I feel all it does is to highlight how utterly waffley my life is anyway.
>
> (Interview 7, January 2007)

There was a suggestion that she achieved 'closure' on earlier parts of her life as a consequence of taking part in the interviews. She appreciated the opportunity to reflect but did not need to return to her early life again and would not repeat the process. One interesting idea she developed in a discussion about learning from narrative was that it could be a process analogous to dreaming, a necessary but transient sorting out of biographical issues:

do you think that's parallel to when we dream, it's a way of sorting out, it's going over something that's bothering the brain and it's sorting out, and then – and the brain does that bit of sorting out in sleep, and when you wake up you may or may not even remember the dream, um and if you do have enough chance to – if you do remember it, you dissect it and you think, 'what on earth was all that about?' . . . but it's your brain sorting out and going back over stuff and sorting out this – possibly just sorting out yesterday's events and tidying it away into its filing cabinet in there.

(Interview 7, January 2007)

Maggie thus presents us with an example of someone who is able to talk in detail about her life but where there is no real evidence that narration functions as a 'site' for learning. As we have mentioned earlier, Maggie makes judgements about her life, but doesn't seem to reflect on it, doesn't seem to ask questions about actions and consequences, about reasons and motivations, about themes and plots. When discussing John Peel we also found little evidence of narrative learning. But whereas there we could link this to the rather scripted character of his narrative and the fact that it provided him with little narrative flexibility, Maggie's life narrative is far from scripted. What, then, might explain the absence of narrative learning in Maggie's case? One suggestion, supported by several aspects of Maggie's story, is that her narration – and perhaps we could also say her mind – doesn't seem to work in a narrative way. Her storying is not chronological or sequential, but neither is it conceptual in the sense in which Bruner makes a distinction between logico-scientific and narrative cognition (see Chapter 1). Maggie's narration seems to present a third option, which, in addition to Bruner's categories, we suggest to refer to as *pictorial* cognition. Maggie talks – and to a certain extent 'thinks' – in images. That is why her accounts are full of detail and complexity but lack sequentiality. That is why her stories are thematic more than chronological. Maggie is able to 'zoom in' and 'zoom out'– as if she is working on a painting of her life – but this depiction does not work as a story. As a result, the kind of reflection that is characteristic of sequential accounts is generally absent in Maggie's stories. At the very same time judgement is very prominent, and again this can be understood in relation to the 'pictorial' character of her accounts, where she can grasp and judge the depiction, the 'Gestalt', as a whole, where she can also judge the relationships between parts and the whole, but where there is no real perception of how these relationships operate and work sequentially, i.e., over time. This is what makes Maggie's case important for this book, as it helps us to see the specific character of *narrative* learning and thereby also the limitations of narration as a form, site or process of learning.

5 Diogenes

Diogenes, a beggar who made his home in the streets of Athens, made a virtue of extreme poverty. He is said to have lived in a large tub, rather than a house, and to have walked through the streets carrying a lamp in the daytime, claiming to be looking for an honest man. He eventually settled in Corinth where he continued to pursue the Cynic ideal of self-sufficiency: a life which was natural and not dependent upon the luxuries of civilisation. Believing that virtue was better revealed in action and not theory, his life was a relentless campaign to debunk the social values and institutions of what he saw as a corrupt society.

(Wikipedia, accessed 24 February 2009)

One of our respondents chose 'Diogenes' as his pseudonym. Diogenes worked for a charity that supports homeless people. On the first occasion we met, he was the warden of a hostel for homeless men and the interview took place in the hostel. The year after, in the year he became 60-years-old, Diogenes was seconded to manage a day centre in a town about 25 miles away from his home. In 2006, he told us that he had agreed to the transfer becoming permanent and he travelled daily to his place of work. It was in the day centre that the other six interviews took place. Diogenes proved to be an articulate participant in the project, able to talk at length during interviews that tended to last for around two hours. He talked eloquently about work and our interviews were able to monitor something of his response to the changes that took place in his life routine as his work role changed. Through this Diogenes provided stories with high narrative intensity and much analysis and evaluation. It was also clear that, unlike some of our participants, he made a clear distinction between his public and private selves in the stories he was prepared to tell. The power of his story-telling was directed in ways that he carefully controlled.

Diogenes

Diogenes was born in 1945. His father had been a businessman of French origin who had stayed in England after military service in the Second World War. He was born in London but brought up in other towns in the south-east of England, going to school in the 1950s and 1960s. Diogenes attended a Catholic school for a period where he was taught by Jesuits and he recalled enthusiasm for subjects like history and archaeology. He visited some of the great Kensington museums and talked of a youthful ambition to become an archaeologist. He attended a grammar school where he was a member of the Air Training Corps (ATC). After completing GCE A level exams, Diogenes went to a redbrick university in the early 1960s to study history and philosophy. He commented how national service had only recently been abolished and how, when thinking about career options, military service was a definite possibility for him, a natural progression for someone with his education and background. His account of that decision-making had rather a sardonic tone:

> What are we going to do? I know, I'll go in the Forces . . . I thought I'll go in the Air Force, I'd been in the Air Cadets, but unfortunately I wore glasses and wouldn't be able to fly so, there we go. So I thought I'd talk to the bloke in the Army. . . . Umm . . ., there's the Intelligence Corps. That sounds interesting, what do they do? Oh, sit round read a lot of magazines, especially pictures with Russian tanks in it and travel around and gather intelligence. Right, . . . Mmm . . ., why not? Okay, we'll give that a whirl.
>
> (Interview 1, November 2004)

Having joined the Intelligence Corps he was soon posted abroad. However, such postings in the 1960s could be to places undergoing political instability and insurgency and Diogenes recounted horrific stories from his experiences in the jungles of Borneo and on the streets of Aden. He described some of his responsibilities at the time:

> . . . the lads had shot some Indonesians, so you got your camera out and you took photographs and you fingerprinted them and you took any relevant documents and unit badges and cut them off the uniform and they smelt rather badly and . . . Umm . . . also there was a ghastly period where they actually wanted the . . . Urm . . . sort of bodies produced . . . the dyak trackers, they had an easy solution actually just cut the hands and heads off and stuff them in a bag because you only wanted the face and the hands for fingerprinting.
>
> (Interview 2, May 2005)

There were stories of casual violence during his posting to Aden:

> . . . things got pretty nasty there. And, you know, there's a little old lady struggling along on a, with a load of wood . . . so an 18-year-old puts a bullet in her head just to break the boredom. Kills an old lady just out gathering wood. Nothing is going to happen to him. No-one's going to bother to enquire, not in those days actually, people were getting shot left right and centre . . . I think if I'd've turned round and reported him I would probably have found a bullet in my head because people turned on each other.
>
> (Interview 2, May 2005)

Diogenes recalled the official silence around these military ventures which affected the stories he could share with family members:

> Nobody really wanted to know so one didn't talk about it. 'So where were you, dear?' 'Umm . . ., Borneo.' 'Oh that was nice, what was it like?' 'Oh it was very nice, actually, Mother, you know, sort of big butter-flies, and orang-utans swinging through the trees and . . . Umm . . . yeah the flora and fauna was wonderful,' you know. 'Wasn't that . . .?' 'Oh no, of course it wasn't dangerous, actually, no, we had a whale of a time. Wonderful.' Well what are you going to tell your mother, you were hacking people's hands and feet, hands and heads off or what have you? Course not, not at all.
>
> (Interview 2, May 2005)

In retrospect, Diogenes reflected that he would have preferred to have undertaken Voluntary Service Overseas (VSO) rather than military service. He was critical of his own formal education, saying he had been ill-prepared for the world he would encounter. However, it seems that one outcome of military service for Diogenes was a sense of how the world should be different: he spoke of his abhorrence of the brutality and violence of war; he was critical of a society that found vast resources for warfare but not for addressing problems of homelessness, that condoned material wealth for some but abandoned others to poverty.

Diogenes served in the army for three years and then undertook VSO in southern Africa, better situated to pursue his ideals of service to fellow human beings. On his return there were two developments that were of lasting significance to the way his life would develop. The first was the discovery that a woman with whom he had been very close before he went to Africa had a young son:

we're talking about an era actually where I suppose one was expected to do the decent thing . . . [pause] we'd had a relationship, I'd then gone off to sort of Africa and that . . . it was just a good relationship but I wasn't actually thinking about getting married . . . She never wrote or anything and told me. We, basically, I sent her a few – a number of nice postcards, a few presents, you know, as you do . . . and it was actually 'Oh,' you know, 'who's the lad?' You know, 'Well, actually he's yours!'

(Interview 6, December 2006)

Diogenes did 'the decent thing' and got married and became father to two more children. The second important development was an encounter with the realities of homelessness in London. Diogenes was able to evoke a critical moment in his life when he decided to dedicate himself to working with homeless people. He described how, in 1972, he tried to locate a family acquaintance who had schizophrenia and who had been evicted from his flat. He went to a night shelter in London where he discovered many homeless people in need of help and his response was to offer to start immediately:

I suppose some people would say (it was) a sort of 'road to Damascus' and anyway, I thought, 'Right you need help,' and well, yeah, so 'Well, when could you start?' so I said, 'Where can I hang my jacket up?'

(Interview 1, November 2004)

The image of Diogenes hanging up his jacket is an important one in the story – he retold it with similar words and greater detail two years later:

So, I thought, 'Well it seems to be pretty worthwhile, so you need people?' I said. 'Well yes, you interested?' I said, 'Well, yes.' They said, 'When could you start?' I said, 'Where can I hang my jacket?' And that was it. That's how I started.

(Interview 6, December 2006)

Following his decision to start working with homeless people, Diogenes spoke of the environment within which he learned the necessary knowledge and skills. He talked of his involvement with the Simon Community in London in the early 1970s and of meeting the founder, Brother Anton, as a charismatic model and inspiration. He recalled how, as a new recruit, he watched other workers to learn about their approach to clients, the language they used, the solutions they found to problems.

You got this group of people clearly with a raft of problems, okay, you're thinking, 'Oh my gosh, you know, what do we do here?' But then you notice the other workers and how they approach and how they work with them, okay and the language they use, the empathy that they have and you think, 'Yeah, that makes sense' or 'No, I don't think I would have said that, I don't think I would have done it that way' but it probably works for them 'cos we're all different actually.

(Interview 3, June 2005)

Diogenes referred to literary and media sources as part of his cultural framework, recalling the impact of television dramas like *Cathy Come Home*. He told stories of meeting paedophiles, prostitutes and abused children in the streets of 1970s London. He mentioned a young girl of 11 who was a prostitute in Kings Cross and recounted the following exchange:

'What the Hell are you doing this sort of thing in London?' 'Well, I might as well be in London getting paid for it as my stepfather getting it for nothing.' 'Did you never thought about talking to your Mum?' 'I don't think my Mum would want to hear, I don't think she'd want to believe me,' so she was no longer a child you know, so there was that sort of stuff.

(Interview 3, June 2005)

He described having to find the personal resources to deal with demanding situations from the start of his involvement with the homeless. A story of one of his earliest experiences in a hostel told how he was responsible for 40 fairly inebriated men while the regular staff went to the pub for a farewell event for their colleague:

I'm looking at four, forty um quite drunk, mostly Irish gentlemen, bless them, thinking 'Oh shit, yeah, yeah, I'm sure I'll be fine, I'm sure I'll be fine.' And um one had to be! So, 'Right okay then guys um so what do we do now?' 'It's, it's nearly time for the meal.' I thought, 'Oh the bastards left me with that! Right, so what we got? I think we'll have a stew day.' So 'Okay then, would a couple of you like to come in the kitchen with me and we'll sort it out, and . . . er . . . right if you'd like to take all the bowls out, if you'd like taking the cutlery and I'll come through and we'll bring the urns in and um can you knock some bread and butter up and all that to go with it?' So you think on your feet and you deal with it. . . . and you get chatting to them while you're doing that so you broke the ice a bit, then you sit down amongst forty people and um quickly lose all your fags, but there you go.

(Interview 7, June 2007)

In several interviews, Diogenes spoke of his work in London and the fact that people he came into contact with lived on the edge of crime; he was aware of drug dealing and pornographic film-making with underage girls. He was also aware of police corruption at the time.

In the 1980s Diogenes worked in the town where he went to university. He helped set up soup kitchens and ran a day centre for homeless people. He worked with a left-wing union firebrand who later became an MP and recalls running a flyposting campaign with him against the Falklands War:

> I designed one actually. Um basically it was a British soldier, actually, with the cross hairs of a sniper's scope round him . . . Most of the arms that the Argentinians used to . . . um . . . use to defend the Falklands, were bought from Britain. So I just put a simple . . . um . . . slogan up there: 'Yesterday we sent the arms, today we send the targets.' It wasn't a great work of art but . . . um . . . it was short punchy and effective.
>
> (Interview 5, July 2006)

In the late 1980s, Diogenes and his family moved to the south-west. His wife was terminally ill and died within a few months of moving, leaving him to look after their three children. During this time he secured a job working in a new hostel for homeless men that was operated by some Christian volunteers and he continues to work for the same charity many years later.

In his recent roles, as warden of a hostel for homeless people and as manager of a day centre, Diogenes has to confront on a daily basis the difficult demands of people who have problems of mental illness, alcoholism, or addiction to street drugs as well as of homelessness. He has many stories that describe the different ways people can find themselves as social outcasts and of the ways in which he has been able to offer support. Sometimes the support enables people to reconstruct purposeful lives for themselves and sometimes it simply gives them reassurance that there are some in society who care about them.

From such stories it is possible to see the construction of a framework for thinking about social and political affairs within which Diogenes undertakes his encounters with homeless people:

> I don't lump them together and say, this group of heroin users, or this group of you know, ecstasy users or this group of pissheads . . . you just see Fred or Joe or Mary or what have you, okay? So, you have to make judgements, but you are not judging them.
>
> (Interview 3, June 2005)

He works within the charity for solutions that are sensitive to the individual circumstances of the service users but he consistently rejects explanations for

those circumstances that are individualised. Instead he attributes homelessness to economic and social conditions in their historical context. However,
the problems that he comes across seem overwhelming:

> We make a difference to some individuals, actually, but it's, it's almost like,
> you know, trying to stick a finger in the dyke, you know, to stop the water
> . . . dealing with that one and there's two more coming over there and
> there's another one . . . here you feel like, I don't know, like these old west-
> erns where you used to see the um the pioneers, you know, pulling their
> wagons in a circle and the Indians riding round and round, actually . . .
> *Everyone* that comes up here has got a problem.
>
> (Interview 5, July 2006)

During the period of our interviews, Diogenes agreed to the transfer within
the charity from being the warden of a hostel to being the manager of a day
centre. The transfer he explained in two ways: first, it enabled him to continue
his everyday work in direct contact with the service users and second, it
enabled him to recapture some of the spirit of his first work with homeless
people: 'I saw coming here was actually going back to my roots which was like,
night shelters, drop-ins, day centres and so on, many, many years ago'
(Interview 3, June 2005).

In one interview, Diogenes was asked whether he was a happy or contented
man, given the extent to which he appeared to have control over his life, but he
replied:

> I'm an extremely unhappy man and an extremely angry man, actually, as
> indeed I think a lot of people should be . . . You know, at the end of the
> day, what the hell am I doing, working with homeless people in 2006? Why
> are there homeless people in 2006? Why are there people actually roaming
> the streets who are clearly unable to look after themselves?
>
> (Interview 5, July 2006)

At the final interview, Diogenes was asked about the connections between his
stories and his identity, how far his narrative is responsible for creating
Diogenes. In response he talked of the changes wrought by experience, noting
particularly that he has become increasingly cynical in his political views. His
answer combined collective factors, in referring to all the people who have
influenced him over the years, with a re-iteration of the sensitivity he considered necessary to respond to individuals:

> [Long pause] I guess Diogenes has been created over the years by thou-
> sands of other people. Um, because of the work I've done and the people

I've worked with, the learning experiences [pause] I mean the last 30 odd years has been a, a learning experience . . . um . . ., . . . um . . . day after day after day because you may have two alcoholics, two drug addicts, two whatever, they have a – they have a, a shared problem, but they are individuals. They have their own life experiences, their own story to tell [pause] so one never lumps a group of people, say, 'right that's a group of alcoholics, that's a group of um heroin addicts, that's a group of whatever,' they're all Fred and Harry and Bill and George and Mike and Nicola and Tracey and [pause] so I guess the trick is [pause] I've got that person, I've got that alcoholic, okay they've got that problem, that problem is shared by many others, but that is that individual.

(Interview 7, June 2007)

Narrative quality

Diogenes' stories are characterised by a high level of narrative intensity. Not only are they detailed and elaborate – they are also full of analysis and evaluation. In one sense it was rather easy for Diogenes to talk about his life but in another sense it was rather difficult. The first interview, for example, lasted about 50 minutes of which the first 20 were an uninterrupted account in which Diogenes explained the background and functioning of the hostel. It was apparent that he had talked about the hostel and the work of the charitable society that supports it frequently in the past and had a well-rehearsed account. He was forthcoming and expansive about his work role but needed questions to encourage him to talk about himself. Subsequent interviews lasted about two hours and contained many stories about Diogenes' earlier life as well as his continuing life in the day centre. He had stories to comprise a public narrative about working with homeless people in a charitable organisation and there were a few stories that gave insight into a more private narrative. The latter gave important clues to understanding the former.

Diogenes' narrative tended to be more thematic than chronological. It has been possible to construct the basic chronology of his life by asking questions and reconstructing data in an appropriately structured manner but it was apparent that, while Diogenes was willing and able to speak at length about themes within his professional role, there were aspects of his life that he did not talk about. He volunteered little about his family and saw little relevance in talking about them. Although he had been a widower since 1991, he said little about the nature of being in such a position.

Self-evidently stories that Diogenes tells are selections from his experience in that he chooses which events of his life will feature in them and which will remain undisclosed. That he was conscious of such decision-making was revealed at the end of the one interview when Diogenes was asked whether he had any questions to ask the interviewer. 'You know, I expect you to kind of bare your soul . . . and I just sit here and listen,' but he insisted he had not 'bared his soul'. He agreed that we had discussed matters that are not part of every-day conversation but he implied there were other aspects of himself that would remain hidden:

> I probably have said a few things that doesn't usually crop up in civilised conversation . . . Umm . . ., and . . . Umm . . . when you walk out the door that will be filed away back in the dark recess and left there, yeah but bare my soul, no I haven't bared my soul, no, no. Oh no.
>
> (Interview 2, May 2005)

Diogenes was able to talk about his experiences in both a personal and an academic framework. Interview transcripts include numerous references to historical events, particularly the Second World War, and Diogenes made sense of his experiences by setting them in a socio-historical context. He referred also to literary sources, to writers like Camus and Sartre, and he referred to media sources as part of his cultural environment, recalling the impact of television dramas like *Cathy Come Home*. In this regard Diogenes was one of the sample of respondents discussed in this book who presented us with a rather theorised version of his life. The quality of analysis and reflection suggests that Diogenes has learned from his narrative – his critical political stance is the outcome of personal experience and theoretical reading that give him his tools for understanding the world and the tasks he undertakes in it.

The identifiable plot of Diogenes' narrative – the organising principle around which he tells stories from his life – is of a quest for greater social justice for homeless people. The story of his recruitment identified a key decision to 'take off his jacket', the story suggested a sudden recognition of an opportunity to be socially useful, and it had direct consequences for Diogenes, his wife and children, and indirectly for the hundreds of people he has worked with subsequently. The decision can also be interpreted as manifesting a disposition to social care that was shaped by the cultural and social structures of which Diogenes was part at that time. His continuing goal is to achieve a better deal, a better understanding in society for homeless people. He is angered by the indifference of others to the problems he encounters everyday and exasperated by the failure of the world to be more humane and more just.

Efficacy: Learning potential and action potential

Diogenes told vivid stories to illustrate how he was recruited into working with homeless people, how he learned his professional skills, how he has worked with different kinds of clients over the years. As we have seen in many quotations, interior discussions took the form of question and answer iteration as well as reconstructed conversations with others:

> At some stage you want to say, you know, 'Okay so you're scoring heroin, you obviously enjoy using heroin?' 'Wrr . . ., I did but not any more.' 'Right so, is there anything you want to do about it, do you want to stop, you know?' 'Umm . . ., where could I go?' 'Well, you could go into a hostel where you could go on a drug programme . . .'
>
> (Interview 3, June 2005)

Although Diogenes retold dialogue-based stories centred on service users, they were not first person narratives in the same way as some other respondents told such stories. A consistent theme through all the interviews was Diogenes' ideal of promoting a better understanding of the conditions of homeless people. He is the principal actor in the stories he tells, someone with a clear ideological identity, while other characters in such stories are rarely more than ciphers – they may serve his belief that in working with homeless people you need to be sensitive to their individual needs, but there was rarely articulation of who such people are, other than as individuals with types of problems that need individualised help.

His stories tended to be well-crafted, with a sense of dramatic structure. For example, there was discussion of Diogenes' role to support the learning of others and he evoked his experiences of hostels and night shelters:

> I remember a case in London actually where . . . er . . . a very, very bright girl actually um, was um was a volunteer with me. I had to go into um into the dormitory to wake up um the guys at eight in the morning and um there were sixteen there actually. Um thirteen got up and three never moved again. Three of them had died during the night, in their sleep. Um I said, 'Well, very sad, they weren't young but at least they didn't die on the streets. They died in the warm,' and what have you. And when I looked around she was gone.
>
> (Interview 7, June 2007)

Diogenes' narrative was important for his self understanding – and in this regard may represent outcomes of narrative learning – but it was not apparent that the narration of these stories in the interviews was itself a learning process. The transcripts suggest that some of his stories were well-rehearsed: he used similar imagery and wording on several occasions such as when telling of 'hanging up his coat' when he started to work with homeless people and when providing lists of first names when asserting the importance of being responsive to individuals. Perhaps such stories had been told on other occasions? Generally, the impression was given that the stories we have in interview transcripts from Diogenes are more or less finished stories: the learning they suggest enables sufficient flexibility in Diogenes' life for him to transfer from one workplace to another but they do not suggest that he is in the process of remaking stories about himself in order to effect the transition. In this respect there are important differences with some of the cases in this book. As we will see in Chapter 9, for example, the stories of Russell Jackson resemble those of Diogenes in that the stories of both have a more or less finished plot that plays a central role in how they analyse, evaluate and story their lives (unlike, for example, someone like Christopher who we present in Chapter 6 and whose storying seems to be more open and ongoing). The difference between Diogenes and Russell, however, is that in Russell's case there is evidence of ongoing learning in relation to his 'plot' whereas in the case of Diogenes it looks more like the learning has been done, conclusions have been drawn, and this has become part of the 'version' he lives. In this regard there are perhaps more resemblances with John Peel, albeit that the 'script' that John's 'lives' is more 'off the peg' while Diogenes' script is clearly the outcome of his own narrative activity.

Diogenes' stories show him to be an idealistic man, although the engine for his ideals and the reasons why they are important to him remain elusive. One possibility is to attribute his idealism to early schooling and his education by Jesuits. Perhaps Diogenes was not comfortable with the advantages of his origins and his professional life has been spent in amelioration of such advantage. The vividness of his stories about military service point strongly to their enduring significance in shaping his understanding of the world. They tell us about his opposition to crude nationalism and to the resolution of international disputes through warfare. Such ideals were realised in the 1960s when Diogenes' military and VSO experiences were powerful factors in forging that framework of values. In the 1970s and the following decades, his social idealism found articulation through an engagement in radical politics and in 'coal face' experiences of supporting homeless people.

We can locate the origins of some of the constructs and ideals that now inform Diogenes' social and political thinking. He opposed the Iraq War, is anti-colonial and sympathetic towards indigenous civilian populations that he sees as the principal victims of modern warfare. He hates violence and any cultural celebration of guns. At the same time he shows understanding and empathy towards those caught up in such conditions. Over the years some of the people he has helped in his work have been men traumatised by their military experiences who are living with the domestic consequences of their military life. He has particular empathy with them. Diogenes has a developed world view that he uses to explain and justify his current role.

It would seem that Diogenes has learned many skills during his life and we can see evidence of his narrative learning. We can secure some insight into the way his narration of stories as dialogues or as interrogative episodes may enable him to reflect on and learn from experience. However, the impression is given that such learning all took place in the past; that his narrative learning has been more or less completed. His knowledge and skills enable him to function in a routine manner and that even enables him to transfer to a different location and use such knowledge and skills in a new environment. However, it looks like there has been little significant 'new' learning for Diogenes despite his transition to a different workplace. This raises important questions about the action potential of Diogenes' narrative learning. Perhaps what we found through the interviews about the decisions Diogenes has made and continues to make about his life, fits with the impression that the story Diogenes recounts – and perhaps we should emphasise: the *public* story that he recounts – is more a finished story than an open, ongoing story. In the stories Diogenes presents himself as someone with clear values and convictions and clear ideas about what he wants and doesn't want, and it is this that centrally informs the way in which he takes decisions, gives direction and responds to opportunities and events. When asked, for example, about how far he had been involved in the decision to be seconded from his hostel to the day centre, he outlined the organisational issues that meant the day centre required someone with experience and sensitivity to take on the manager's role. He welcomed the challenge:

> Although I am 60-years-old, or coming up to 60 actually, I needed that challenge. Umm . . ., I'm not being big-headed now I think I've started to find in the last year or so a bit too easy, a bit too easy in the hostel, . . . Umm . . ., because after a number of years I've got it pretty well off pat.
>
> (Interview 3, June 2005)

He suggested he had become complacent in doing much the same job for 14 years, had become accustomed to the routines of hostel management, and was able to identify routine solutions for most of the problems presented by the service users.

> I thought it was actually quite a good idea to actually sort of go back to one's roots and I saw coming here was actually going back to my roots which was like, night shelters, drop-ins, day centres and so on, many, many years ago.
>
> (Interview 3, June 2005)

There is thus rather a nostalgic reference to earlier identity.

Another discussion centred on Diogenes' reluctance to take a senior role in the management of the charity. There is no doubt he is well respected for his experience and expertise in the field – indeed, it emerged that there had been a suggestion that Diogenes should be nominated for an honour, a proposal he quickly quashed. He is eminently capable of a managerial or a policy-making role. Nonetheless, he asserted his preference for continued close contact with service users and justified his resistance to joining senior managers or policy makers because of their tendency to become preoccupied with 'units' rather than 'people':

Have you ever been tempted or interested in that sort of managerial side rather than the warden side?

No, because I've always tended to find myself happier working at – as they say at the coal face, hands on, not literally of course, but you know hands on with the, with the service users, yeah . . . I've written handbooks and manuals, all sorts of stuff actually, you know, how to deal with stuff and all that. Um . . ., you – it can be I mean I've seen it happen with colleagues who've moved on.

. . .

That's not something that's ever appealed to you?

No, because it's so easy to lose touch, and people do. And I'll sort of say, – I've sat at meetings where people of a certain level have been discussing the homeless in the same way as somebody in business would, would, would talk about how many tonnes of sugar they're importing, or how many cars they're bringing in. It's, it's – can then become a commodity. This is what the organisation I work with does . . . it's quite scary. It's almost like listening to transcripts of um, conversations the Nazis have actually. They never spoke about, 'we are shipping twelve hundred Hungarian Jews,' actually, it was units . . .

But arguably you can make a bigger difference when you're in that sort of level of management?

. . . Of course you make a difference. The policy makers . . . decide what speed you can drive your car to go home tonight, what you can or can't do, to a large degree. Um, it's a question of whether you would like to be up there with them, or, or dealing with it at grass roots level where somebody comes in saying, 'I slept out last night, it was effing cold, I wish I had a sleeping bag.' 'Well I'll see what I can do to get hold of a sleeping bag for you.' To me that's, or, 'I'm really hungry. I haven't eaten for two days. I've had to rummage in dustbins, for a hot meal.' To me that surely is yep . . .

(Interview 4, January 2006)

Diogenes insisted that he was happier working directly with service users. Although he said he was not a Christian, he referred wryly to the direct action of Jesus Christ:

> I don't think Christ was actually up with the policy makers. He may have been with the supreme policy maker, but he wasn't, he wasn't with the Council of Elders at the Jewish Temple or at Herod's Court. I mean he could have wiggled his way into that! Maybe he could have, you know, maybe he should have become a, I don't know, a Roman citizen and gone to Rome and tried to affect things at that level?
>
> (Interview 4, January 2006)

At a subsequent interview Diogenes made the point that his children had grown up and left home and he has responsibilities only for himself. He argued that his material needs were small; repeatedly he had expressed his impatience with contemporary materialism and his contempt for media trivia and asserted that he saw himself as 'A bit of a minimalist, personally, you know' (Interview 5, July 2006).

In considering the action potential of Diogenes' learning, his life story shows us someone who has been able and continues to be able to exert control over and give direction to his personal life. He achieves agency in his work for others, he is able to create circumstances in which they can achieve change in their lives if they decide to do so. Although his ideals remain constant, there has been a process of disillusion with the direction of change in the world. Diogenes is true to ideals forged many years ago and unwilling to change himself for present circumstances; he has an identity that remains detached from the materialism and trivia of everyday life. But it becomes evident that there is a price to pay for such integrity, and that a capacity to produce an elaborated narrative is no guarantee of elaborated agency of the kind we will see, for example, in the cases of Christopher and Russell Jackson.

6 Christopher

Christopher is another example of someone whose life story is characterised by a high level of narrative intensity and where the predominant mode of narration is on the analytical and evaluative side of the spectrum much more than on the descriptive end. However, even in those cases where there are emplotted, analytical and evaluative stories with high narrative intensity, there are still important differences in terms of the learning potential – for example, as we have seen in the previous chapter, about whether the learning is completed or ongoing – and also with regard to the action potential. In contrast to Diogenes, Christopher presents us with narrative and narration that is much more an ongoing learning process; one, moreover, with a clear potential for action.

Christopher

Christopher was born in 1942 into a middle-class family in southern England. There was, he believes, a 'golden time' (Interview 8, June 2007) for the first 30 months of his life.

> There's a picture of my mother holding me as a very young child, when I was quite newly born, and there's a photograph she'd written on the back to send to someone, this is, this is my new child Christopher, something like isn't he sweet, or isn't he lovely or something, written on the back. So I think at some, when I was very young I was loved, very much, by my mother.
>
> (Interview 3, December 2005)

There was, in the photograph,

> . . . real warmth, and the way she'd written this on the back. It was obviously genuine you know.
>
> (Interview 3, December 2005)

Fifteen months after the birth of Christopher, his mother gave birth to another son. By the time Christopher was two-and-a-half-years-old, his parents parted and divorced. Up to that point, although he thinks he may be able to remember 'terrible rows' between his parents, his 'myth' is that this was a period of 'safety'.

> That's the feeling. It was safe up to there . . . I feel I was loved, and I feel as though I know, I know what it feels like to have been loved, and I think if I hadn't known that, I could be a drug addict, I could be a delinquent, I could be a criminal, I don't know what I could be, but because of that, that redeems me. That's my feeling.
>
> (Interview 8, June 2007)

His mother remarried; Christopher and his step-father were unable to build a close father–son relationship. His mother ultimately sank into alcoholism and agoraphobia.

> . . . I can remember the daily grind of living in a place where, which was out of joint, and where love was not, a generous commodity, it wasn't there on tap. And mother had to hide in a way, had to be sort of just through there in order to be loving, not be in the room with you . . .
>
> (Interview 7, August 2006)

Of his mother he says,

> I see her a bit like a spider in a way, sitting at the centre of a web and all the threads go out to all the, all the, so she didn't come in and *actively* encourage, but you felt the sort of the pull of the threads when things were done right or whatever, because my step-father was so dominant in the house, you know, he ruled it with a rod of iron . . . he ruled with a rod of iron and my mother I think rather retreated, so she, she did it by throwing her threads all around the house and she would just gently pull on a thread when you were doing it right. I don't, she never, I don't think she ever came up and, actually encouraged. I don't associate mothers doing that. I associate fathers perhaps. That's a fatherly role which I never got.
>
> (Interview 3, December 2005)

He was sent to a PNEU (Parents' National Education) prep. school. PNEU schools are based on the philosophy of Charlotte Mason. Although Christopher did not tell of his time at this or subsequent schools (other than that it was reported that he was a 'trial and a tribulation'), two aspects of the school's philosophy are striking. First, Mason believed that it was important to tap into the 'talking resource' of children, considering their talk to be the art of narration. She had the notion that narration invited a child's personality to become part of her/his learning process. Second, she believed that in a structured, supported way, it was best to leave children to learn 'naturally', sometimes with little or no intervention from adults. PNEU schools have the motto 'I am, I can, I ought, I will'.

From about the age of eight, when he discovered puppets, Christopher, it seems, began a life-long occupation in puppetry. At primary school, when Christopher was seven or eight-years-old, a fellow pupil

> . . . had a little articulated doll . . . I really wanted it . . . it was a little jointed figure and I loved that little jointed figure that this person had . . . I think the fact that it had little joints, I loved the fact that you could move it. So it wasn't just like a teddy bear, it was also something you could move and you could change its aspect, and I think that there was already probably the beginnings of wanting to imprint myself on the outer world through using objects . . . it feels like I was taking a seed in from those early adorable objects, that I was taking something inside myself, planting a seed, I mean that little figure, that little Hrvnek figure, which was this adorable, he had clogs on and was a little Czechoslovakia, and, and I think Pinocchio, Pinocchio has that, the little jointed legs and everything, and I think I adored that. And I think it was like something, almost taking the seed in to me.
>
> (Interview 4, January 2006)

By the age of nine or ten he

> . . . was clearly passionate about puppets . . .
>
> (Interview 7, August 2006)

He learned that he could, through his puppets,

> . . . articulate living, of course a puppet isn't living, I know that, but I could bring it to life. I learnt that quite soon by my little toy Muffin the Mule. So, I was, I knew that there was this love, love affair with these puppets . . .
>
> (Interview 4, January 2006)

Puppetry, at this early age

> . . . gives me all my quirkiness and my Mythicness and it seems to satisfy a lot of the needs that I seemed to have as a human being at that time. I think

the fact that puppets are quirky and strange and jerky and cheeky and all the things, in a way I've put a lot of my stuff into that . . . So I discover something very important at that stage, which is going to put me on a trajectory . . .

(Interview 8, June 2007)

But it is a trajectory somewhere, rather than a definitive goal to be attained. There is ambivalence:

. . .when I was probably twelve or something, I used to, in the . . . library they had a section just right at the bottom for puppets some things on puppets, and it was right at the bottom of the shelves so you could sit on the floor and enjoy the books, it was great, because you could be just very intimate with these little books which I loved . . . one of them was of this puppeteer . . . it had lots of photographs of his puppets and I remember thinking, just loving these puppets, the beauty of them, the craft of, the craft of them, and thinking wouldn't it be wonderful if I could make puppets like that one day . . .

(Interview 1, October 2005)

From about the age of nine Christopher began to be involved in activities which supported puppetry. There is a

. . . list of things which I did in my teens, all to do with theatre and around the stuff that I do now . . . I think it's remarkable, when I look at this list which I've brought along, of the things, how, you know, out of nothing, I, what I did with no tutor or anything, you know, I didn't have any tutor at all . . . at the age of eleven, twelve, thirteen and I was putting together a whole career, a whole way of life.

(Interview 7, August 2006)

. . . I know at that point, from that point on, right the way through my teens and really right the way through my life . . . I set myself on a trajectory which I really worked at . . . there's a huge list of things which I . . . projects that I did. And it feels like I was *really* working hard towards it, so it feels like that at the, really working hard to, to put something, to create something, of, of my situation.

(Interview 7, August 2006)

While there was a clear path in Christopher's vocation, he commented that this was far less so in his relationships with others.

... in interaction with people, I just had *no* language, no way of, of being with people, I was shy, I was anxious, . . . er . . ., . . . Erm . . ., and I was . . . Erm . . ., I sort of cut myself off . . .

(Interview 2, November 2005)

At school Christopher was exploring relationships with boys and girls. At art college:

I had a girlfriend there . . . and we had some pretty great adventures . . . Exploring being straight or being gay. I mean, I knew at school that I loved, I don't know if I should be saying this, but I loved the sexual encounters with the boys there. I'm sure a lot of kids do. Anyway, I did. But then I was, I was exploring being straight, you know, I had this girl . . . friend, and we had all kinds of adventures and it was sexual too . . . I think I was sort of learning about one-to-one relationships.

(Interview 8, June 2007)

Following the death of his mother Christopher found himself in 'a terrible mess' (Interview 2, November 2005). Already in a relationship, he met and fell in love with a gay Irish Catholic. He let the relationship run its course and, per-haps for the only time, might have been prepared to abandon his work for the sake of the love affair. Ultimately, Christopher found himself living alone and chose to take a course of action which was to result in him moving on from the shy, anxious phase of his life, but this plan of action only occurred when Christopher was in his thirties. It involved intensive therapy and though he no longer attends regular therapy he does elect to take part in therapeutic work-shops and has found a co-counsellor recently to help him work through his story.

During the course of our interviews with Christopher his long-term partner left him for another man.

So part of what I want to do now is to, not exactly reinvent myself, but rediscover myself as a, as it were, in quotes, single man. You know, maybe I'll have a partner again in a little while, but maybe I'll, you know, I want to know what it is now to do, to do this . . . it feels like I have a, quite a, a lot of, abilities, so it feels like . . . Erm . . ., I maybe it's having the courage to wait and discover where, where it is to go now.

(Interview 1, October 2005)

Not only did his partner leave him but there was a disagreement with a long-standing friend that resulted in the breakdown of the friendship; another friend of many years became ill and died. Christopher found himself once more alone, as in childhood.

> So here I am in a temporary accommodation with someone who's very nice to me, very . . . er . . ., supportive, but not a friend in the sense I've only met him through this accommodation, and I'm about to buy a new flat and it feels like it's a big, restarting of my life in a way. In a new way, without a partner and without two very important people in my life. And I'm, sometimes I think what is that, telling me, what is life, inviting me to do next. That's a learning.
>
> *And have you come up with any kind of answer to that?*
>
> My feeling at the moment, it's quite strong and clear, is that it's almost like I just need to contain all these things in myself and wait. I do feel that. It's almost like it has to be, like in a, like in a pot or a bowl inside me. It's not cooking, it's just sitting, and . . . Erm . . ., I, it would be wrong to pre-empt it in any way. I feel there's a lot of stuff there that, if I'm patient and can have the strength to just contain it, hold it, could be very rich. But it's not easy because it's lonely, being without these people and without what was my home, you know. So it feels, [pause] it feels emotional, really.
>
> (Interview 2, November 2005)

Temporarily this lonely state

> . . . feels a bit like the project I'm on at the moment, . . . Erm . . ., it's like, exploring life alone.
>
> (Interview 5, March 2006)

> . . . my whole life is changed . . . it just feels like I'm, I'm literally finding a new Christopher. Not a new, a new Christopher, . . . er . . ., no, not a new Christopher because, . . . Erm . . ., obviously, I think the Christopher is the same, but it's like a new way, a new, it feels like a new chapter of my life has opened up and I'm, I'm starting this new chapter, and it's, the pages in the future have no writing on them. Whereas I think up to the point at which I separated, the pages on the next few pages did have writing on them, because I had a projection of where I would be going, what life would be like. But now I don't . . . it feels like I've become quite porous to life now, and I feel like I'm, I'm soaking in life again, and it feels like, . . . Erm . . ., in order to, to, to give myself a maximum opportunity to, to move into the next place. That's what it feels like . . . I feel that I'm open, at the moment, and that feels like . . . er . . ., there are places where I can look at again which I haven't perhaps looked at . . . I'm much more open to, to things

emerging out of whatever is, whatever is there in front of me or around me.

(Interview 6, June 2006)

. . . it's lonely. It's alone, being alone. I find that challenging. And part of me really wants to find a partner, soon, quick. But part of me feels that that is not what I should be doing. Part of me feels that I need to . . . Erm . . ., I'm sure it would be possible to find someone, but part of me feels that it's important to . . . have the experience of being alone . . . it feels like, if I was to run into another relationship and live with someone, I would be missing out, I would be escaping from something very important.

Which is?

[pause] Facing up to the fact that I feel ultimately completely alone. Absolutely alone, and, and this has some, and I think of death . . . I do think that that is the one thing that we experience utterly alone is the experience of death, and I feel that, so maybe I am experiencing some kind of experience of death at the moment. It's the death of a relationship. And I think in some ways it feels like the death of a life, in a way, I feel that [pause] I was thinking just this morning I think, as I was getting up, I was thinking how many unfinished projects I have in my life, masses of unfinished projects, and I thought, well, maybe my life is an unfinished project. Maybe at the end of my life it will be an unfinished project.

(Interview 7, August 2006)

By the next interview, however, he had a new boyfriend whom he actively invited into his life.

. . . I feel I've reclaimed something of my zip.

(Interview 8, June 2007)

Christopher's story ultimately becomes, in part at least, one of a search to encompass his spiritual needs within his occupation/vocation. When young

. . . I feel that when, in those very early years, you know, when, in the second half of my first decade, between whatever, five and nine, that I was, I was quite monkish, I think . . . I was a sort of bit like a little monk, I think . . . I didn't fit in. I know monks do fit in, but I, isolated myself from a world which I didn't fit in like monks do. You know, they come away from the world in order to live away from, apart from a busy world or whatever, and I feel I did do that a bit. But it was through necessity because I couldn't think of any alternative. So maybe I learnt something about, about that, about being resourceful alone.

(Interview 7, August 2006)

. . . all my life I've, I've been intrigued and fascinated and tempted by the, by the solitary life, by the life of a monk or a hermit. I always found that very beautiful.

(Interview 1, October 2005)

When Christopher was established as a puppeteer he began to introduce into his work first demonic, phallic and shadow figures; this was followed by a period of work on saints.

. . . the thing of doing stories of saints is something which, I think is look-ing, it's, it's actually looking for the saint within oneself . . . looking for that purity, that . . . Erm . . ., quality of the miraculous, that I think we all have and that I think I see in puppets the simplicity of the puppets has that saintly quality, it has also the opposite, it has the . . . diabolic as well. And that's the shadow side which is and I have that too.

(Interview 1, October 2005)

By his early thirties Christopher

. . . was trying at the time to, practise spiritual, you know, I was trying to meditate, I was doing Tai Chi, I was, reading a lot, trying to do a lot of kind of, I began going to church as well, I was trying to, do some kind of spiri-tual practice, but I was very spasmodic, I'd do a bit of this then I'd not do it, then I'd oh I'm meant to be doing that, you know, and one day I thought well why not, why not do the, put the, one thing I do at, on a regular basis is work on my, my art. I don't have any difficulty in doing that, I don't lapse with that . . . why not put the two together, so say the spiritual is in har-mony with the work, it's, after all life is only a certain length and maybe there isn't time to do all these other things and maybe one has to sort of dovetail, that was what I was thinking.

(Interview 2, November 2005)

Now in his mid-sixties, Christopher reflects on life plans, trajectories, quests and goals. He believes that everybody has a 'trajectory' for their life.

I don't think trajectory is something you decide, I think it's something that, that happens to you from, almost the moment of birth. Has to do with karma and all these things, it has to do with that, that it's not, I don't actually believe in predestination or, or that, but I, I think there is something *in* the power of the trajectory and I do think that, I don't believe that people don't have trajectories.

(Interview 7, August 2006)

They say that, that every family, every child is put on a trajectory of life, you know, I think it's a bit like the family pull the bow back with the child and aim the arrow in a certain trajectory and then let it go, with the child, and then the rest of the life of the child has to do with that trajectory, that the parents have sort of established. I think there's a lot of truth in that.

(Interview 3, December 2005)

So you see it more that it's life doing something to you rather than you doing something to life?

No, I think it's both ways, because I am also travelling. It's not as though, . . . Erm . . ., I'm travelling but I'm actually travelling through, through life. So I don't feel that it's just life doing something to me, I don't think I do. No, I don't. [pause] I mean, maybe at one level it would be better if I did, then I would be more, . . . Erm . . ., more free to, for life to offer challenges which maybe I haven't decided. Maybe the fact that one has a, a sort of plan, an ambition, in a way limits life perhaps a little bit, I don't know. And I think if you don't have any kind, if I don't have any kind of ambition I would probably be a drunk sitting beside the road or someone walking around with hardly any clothes on and a bag of, of greasy possessions, you know, I mean, I feel, I feel, part of me feels there's a, quite a fine thing between, you know, being . . . Erm . . ., together and able to function, and being not able to function at all. I feel that quite closely. That's what I feel whenever I see someone who is in a hard-up state, I, I just feel there but for the grace of God go I . . .

(Interview 5, March 2006)

But Christopher also feels a need to *do* something about difficult situations.

. . . I don't think I've ever felt that I was born to be . . . Erm . . ., a criminal or a, I don't think I have, although I have, you know, when I walk past someone sitting on the street, you know, with a begging bowl, I do genuinely feel there but for the grace of God, I really do, I feel you're only that far away from me, I'm only that far away from you, I know where you are, but I also now know, it's like Christ's thing, you know, . . . Erm . . ., whatever it is, heal thyself, no, what is it, pick up thy bed and walk, and I know what that, I know what the difference between collapsing on the street

and asking for money, and getting up and walking on in life is. And I sometimes feel, when I see these people, just like saying, just get up and walk, *go*.

(Interview 8, June 2007)

I think I've always wanted to make the very, to say make the best of my life
it doesn't quite feel like that because I don't feel like it's a, it's a, a plan I
could draw up, it's like, it feels like what I want to do is, is, it's a bit like when
you go into the sea, and you push and you feel, against the water walking
out, and you feel you're pushing in through, through the water out to sea
as you walk into the deeper water. That's what I feel a little bit, life with me,
it's like I'm wading into life, so I couldn't really say exactly where it, where
it, or what it is but it feels like what I've, what I've always wanted to do
is, is take the next step into that, that ocean or whatever it is, it feels a bit
like that.

(Interview 5, March 2006)

. . . I mean, my journey seems to be toward some kind of fulfilment, some
kind of completeness, some kind of togetherness with myself and with
the world.

(Interview 9, July 2007)

Christopher's story is one of unification, 'wholeness' and transcending worldly
living. He uses his puppets as:

. . . some kind of cement, not a cement, some kind of linking factor, that
they can take on any role, I can make, I feel now that the puppets [beep]
but the puppets, it's almost like they can, I feel now overtly that the
puppets are part of me, you know, that they are fragments of my psyche
. . . I've never, ever wavered from puppets, I've never wanted to do, I've
never, ever been, had the feeling, I want to do something else, *ever*, ever,
ever. And I know people who have started on something, say oh we gave
that up. Sometimes I've thought, recently I've thought, well maybe there
will come a time when I will no longer do the puppets. I will do something
else, I will be beyond the puppets or something . . . But you see, if I've
dropped out, and I have occasionally, I've thought, well, I'll do something,
I'll do music or I'll do whatever, I've ploughed it back in, so once I've
dropped out, I then put it back in the puppet thing and turn it over again,
it's like riches, enriches the soup, the puppetry soup.

But when you drop out to do something like music?

I suppose it's within the puppetry story . . . it's always had the feeling that
it'll be useful in the puppets later on, but like there, because I've, I, I think
I've said, I don't want to end my life with regrets, thinking, I wish I'd done

this or, so I did study the harp, I thought at the time, you know, I'll learn to play the harp, used to practice for an hour every day for quite a long period and at the back of my mind I thought, this'll be useful for the puppets, but it was also that I felt I'm *really* getting stuck into something I've always wanted to do. I think with the singing now, I feel there's a bit of that, too, it's not just for the puppets, it's partly just for me. But I've never . . .

For you for what, though?

Because I have a voice. And I've got a good voice.

And what about with the harp?

I suppose it's an odd instrument and it moves me very much, I love it, I love the sound, the idea of stroking, plucking, playing the strings. But I've never been disloyal to the puppets in the sense I've never said, well, that's it, I've given you up.

(Interview 9, July 2007)

Asked if he has ever doubted his return to puppetry when he has taken time out, he responds:

Never, never, never. Never, never, never. But just recently I've thought, well, there may be a time when the puppets, I no long do the puppets any more. I've always thought I'd always have a workshop 'til the day I die. And just occasionally I've thought, well, maybe I won't need one 'til the day I die. I don't know what that means. Maybe I'll find some way of transcending the puppets. But at the moment, I feel that there's so much juice, so much richness in my relationship with them and, and what we offer each other, what they offer me and what I offer them in terms of my, it has been my career, but also in terms of my personal development.

(Interview 9, July 2007)

He feels that he has brought together his artistic and spiritual journeys though he has been less successful in integrating his relational with his occupational/spiritual aspects. In his current relationship he feels this may be about to change.

Narrative quality

It is not difficult to discern the high level of narrative intensity of Christopher's stories. Not only are they detailed and elaborate, they also have depth in that they not simply provide much detail at a descriptive level, but are characterised by constant analysis, interpretation, sense-making and evaluation. In this regard the narrative quality of Christopher's stories is significantly different from the narratives we have discussed in the chapters so far. For Christopher 'making sense' of his life, figuring out what is going on and why it is going on is an ongoing project. It is not something that was triggered by the interviews – although the interviews did provide him with additional opportunities for articulation and reflection – but is very much part of who Christopher is and how he is continuously trying to make sense of his life. Although we might say that Christopher's life story has a clear plot, for example, the conviction that there is a 'trajectory' as Christopher calls it, which is not an arbitrary choice about how to lead one's life, but more like a kind of life theme that is there to be found and to be acted upon – what seems more appropriate here is to say that Christopher's narratives are characterised by *ongoing emplotment*. Indeed, in the very last interview Christopher begins to reassess his identity as an artist and raises some deep questions about his sense of self and the direction of his life so far.

> I think that one of the big things is that the whole art thing is now being questioned for the first time in my life. You know, the idea of my being an artist, what it is to be an artist, and it comes back to a lot of the things in our interviews, where I've talked about the reason for being an artist, and your marvellous thing of the [pause] oh, what's it called, the thing into gold, lead into gold.
>
> *Alchemy.*
>
> Alchemy. And I do think that's what happened to me. And I think, I think, . . . Erm . . ., I think I've used my whole art throughout my life, I've used it as an escape hatch, as a place to go when things got really hard. And I think in there has been, although I *do* think I have a *really*, a real vocation, I really think I have something to offer as an artist, I really do think I'm a true artist, I also think that through that I have actually missed out on a tremendous lot, or somehow side-stepped commitment to a lot of things that aren't to do with art.
>
> . . . and it feels like a lot of all that needs to be assessed, the whole thing of what I've been doing with my life. There's a little bit of grieving because I'm 65 now and am thinking well, and I'm thinking also there's a lot of work, I've got trunks of puppets that are unfinished projects that I've gone into *whole*-heartedly, you know, I've probably told you that there was one play I did, I did almost the complete range of puppets which were about four feet high and I then decided they were all too big, so I started to carve the *whole* lot at about half their size, you know, and all these are in trunks because I never finished the project in the first place, in the end anyway.
>
> *And what are you saying that makes you feel?*

What I think I'm saying is that, that I think [pause] that me being, my art, my being an artist is part of, was part of my stumbling in life, or *is* part of my stumbling in life, and . . . Erm . . ., so it's not surprising there are unfinished projects, things that I've sort of gone into, is it this place, do I, is this the place, it's almost like *is this* the place where it will *really* happen?

Ongoing emplotment not only means that Christopher is continuously trying to make sense of his life and is trying to figure out what is going on – something which obviously requires analysis and evaluation. Through his narration he is also *creating* meaning and making his life meaningful. This means that Christopher's life story takes on a meaning unique to himself, although he draws on the scripts of others to weave his own yarns. There is not an 'off the peg' script that Christopher simply adopts; the life story is his unique creation and it is intimately connected with how he leads his life. In this regard his narrative is not simply retrospective and reflective; it is also prospective and pro-active. This brings us to questions about learning and action.

Efficacy: Learning potential and action potential

Christopher's life is ubiquitous with learning. He appears to lap up learning, partly building on the foundations of his PNEU schooling, but always in the service of his story of becoming a great puppeteer. Learning for any other reason is 'sleepwalking'. He has taken formal courses, sought out experts and reads extensively. Throughout his later childhood he learned, deliberately through 'play' and reading; in his teens he sought out opportunities to learn a broad range of theatre skills through participation. He learned in his apprenticeship and later took a formal drama course; learned to play musical instruments, to write music, to sing. But he also thrived on learning from his friends and partners, about the arts and culture from around the world and yearns for intellectual relationships that allow him to pit himself against others' minds. He is deeply spiritual, but rather than engaging with the script of traditional religion, Christopher weaves his own narrative of spirituality, integrating aspects of tradition with his own life story. He has also learned about personal development through therapy, reading and therapeutic workshops. Yet again he has also developed his own means of personal development through his puppetry story.

Narrative is clearly a major part of Christopher. His work as a puppeteer ensures that he practises storytelling within his occupation, adopting, adapting and creating storylines for his inanimate friends. He views therapy as an especially important part of his development and his creativity. It is interesting to note that his choices are not 'talking therapies' which he does not feel appropriate. He selects those where he is able to enact as well as narrate his inner world. This he does also through the stories he uses with his puppets. Through narration at work, in therapy, and with himself, it would seem, Christopher is able to create a notion of unity in a life that has not always been unified. He can create hooks by which to pull himself out of the tumultuous periods in his life. But he may also be creating a 'narrative prison', where he is unable to connect fully with 'reality'.

From this angle we can say that the kind of narration that Christopher has been involved in throughout his life – narration that is characterised by intensity and depth, analysis, reflection and judgement, and by ongoing emplotment – functions indeed as a 'site' for learning, that is, a site where Christopher tries to figure out what is going on and tries to make meaning out of his narrations and reflections. But Christopher's narration is not just a site for learning without consequences. Christopher does not only narrate the story; he also plans and acts. Christopher's is therefore an example of narration that not only has a high learning potential but also a high action potential. This partly has to do with the particular quality of his narration – the ongoing emplotment – yet it is also clear that this hangs together with his belief that there is a 'trajectory', that life is meaningful and that it is his task to find out what the meaning, plan and trajectory for him *is*. His narration both reflects and enacts this belief.

Christopher appears to have created much of his script for himself but there are societal scripts which influence the telling. He draws on the societal scripts of the 1960s and 1970s, especially around art and spirituality (he comments about the influences coming especially from America). He draws on Eastern as well as Western ways of knowing, on a range of religious scripts from which he creates his own telling. He has had much exposure to psychotherapeutic scripts and these appear strongly in his story and may explain why he dwells so much on the impact of his early years. Christopher's narrative and narration show how a more personally crafted narrative emerges. The personal element lies not so much in the carte blanche creation of a narrative, more in the systematic bricolage by which a personal mosaic is created of many different socially available scripts. In his case this personal narrative also provides a vocational pathway and livelihood throughout his life. But even here the pursuit of personal autonomy has its limits for we see towards the end of his life considerable rumination on how a personally crafted narrative can itself imprison as well as liberate a life.

Although Christopher's narrative has its own limitations it clearly illustrates how narrative learning can lead to the definition of a 'course of action'. In this case the course of action provided a whole pathway to vocational purpose and economic livelihood but it is more than that – it is an existential axis on which his whole life turns and in a real sense depends.

7   Paul Larsen

At one level the stories that Paul Larsen told us about his life are quite similar to those of Christopher, in that they are characterised by a high level of narrative intensity, by detailed analysis and evaluation and by a continued engagement with questions of meaning, interpretation and understanding. In this regard Paul's case can be seen as another example of narrative learning in action. Where Paul's narrative is different, however, is in the things that Paul is able to do with his narrative and narration. Looking at the action potential of Paul's narrative and narration reveals some interesting differences compared to Christopher's case – differences that add to the palette of modes and ways of narrative learning that we are exploring in these chapters. Eliciting an initial life story for Paul took a different route to most in the Learning Lives project in that he chose to write a 'journal' about his life which complemented the work he was doing as part of his own doctoral research. The 'journal' has been used in lieu of a first interview.

Paul Larsen

Paul was born in 1949 in a rural area of Norway. Partly his family were farmers and fishing folk, but his father also worked as a skilled worker in the manufacturing industry. It was a job that took him away from home a great deal; on his return he was 'like a visitor'. Paul's mother and older sister were the 'rulers' of the home, a home that had strong affiliation to the Lutheran Free Church with its strictures against frivolity and pleasure in life. Within his story Paul portrays an image of his being a 'mistake'.

> I was born the last of four children, half-an-hour after my twin brother. They say I wasn't expected and therefore had no clothes to wear when I came into the world.
>
> (Interview 1, October 2004)

I always thought that Norway was, ... er ..., it was a mistake I was born in Norway. It was a big mistake. I shouldn't have been born there. So I've very, I was very close to dying when I was a baby, but I survived by a strike of luck or what you can call it, depending on the perspective you use. I wasn't, I wasn't supposed to, to be born there. [laughs]

(Interview 4, February 2006)

In interview 5 he reflects on a therapy session he had where the therapist had led him back to 'memories' of his very early life.

... but I remember my mother told, told about I was going, I was about to die ... I was turning blue, dark blue, and there was a nurse who put a piece of soap in my, in my back, and phew! And then she [the therapist] said, maybe, maybe that's an important point, maybe your father was there, maybe he, maybe he, maybe you sensed that he wasn't happy or, because I talked about, he wasn't prepared, he wasn't prepared I was coming. I asked him when I was in Norway, last year, did you know you were having twins when we were born? Pooh, he said, pooh, men, we don't, we didn't, we weren't told anything. So he wasn't prepared to have two. And as I told you, he was away a lot, and he struggled ... er ..., probably with earning enough money for his family, he always bought second-hand shoes, we were very poor. And this therapist, she said, I think you weren't wanted, you weren't, ... er ..., wanted even when you were made, she said. That was a very cruel thing to say, but I think she knew I was, able to take it. I just found it interesting. So maybe that's an idea I have used in this conversation that I was born into the wrong place. I shouldn't be, but why are people born into places they shouldn't have been?

(Interview 5, December 2006)

Paul was – by his account – a 'smothered' child. His mother, an anxious, fearful woman, wrapped him in 'itchy woollen' clothes which he hated.

And then you feel choked as a child then because, you want a life of your own from you're three years I think, three or four-years-old.

(Interview 4, February 2006)

But for all the 'smothering', there was also a missing connection.

My mother she was singing ... just as if she wasn't in the room. She had a kind of voice which was out of the room ... she was singing as she, as if she wasn't in the kitchen. She made a cathedral ... she was, maybe that's, there is connection to daydreaming there because she was, she was carrying herself away through the song, I guess she was. That's, that's the way I remember her voice . . . my mother, she sang in the kitchen, but she didn't sing *with* us, she was in her cathedral. She didn't, she didn't include her, she didn't take us on her knee and sang with us . . . People who have been sitting on their mother's knee . . . I wasn't sitting on my mother's knee as other people were. She was in her own space. So I say that singing was apart, from the life.

(Interview 4, February 2006)

His father, when he was at home, was a man of ambivalence. Paul tells of his fear of his red-faced father, of being beaten by him for minor crimes committed; the other side to a mild man who used to entertain the children playing guitar or mandolin and singing.

. . . sometime I was, physically punished, and I hated my father for, quite, a couple of years at least, if you can say so. Strong feelings against so strong him that I, I thought feelings against I must have hated him then. [pause]

(Interview 2, November 2004)

By the time Paul was ten or eleven, the idea of him becoming a teacher had been mooted within the family. At school his teacher spoke in general terms about children going to university, and Paul:

. . . started thinking myself, could that be me? What is university? . . . I thought about it when I was ten years. What is this university . . . I started having an idea of myself of how good I was in school work and tasks the teachers used to give.

(Interview 3, June 2005)

In the home Paul suffered from asthma and allergies.

. . . I wanted to get out of the house. It was connected to, atmosphere, homely atmosphere, to untold things. You could forget about that when we were in the street and playing cricket or what it was, with the boys. Forget, forgot about everything. Rowing and fishing and swimming or whatever it was, was gone. But back to home. [pause] So this idea about home as a nice and, and . . . er . . . , always nice to get home, it's not true for me.

(Interview 4, February 2006)

Paul found an escape, through his childhood, from the home he appears to have loathed. Paul was sent to Sunday school where he was befriended by the teacher who taught him to play melodies on the accordion.

> . . . music was maybe music, at that Sunday school was was sort of real [pause] a sort of, balm would you say, it was soothing, it was, it was soothing me into, where I could be free of, and that was the other side, punishment was [pause] the scary side. And, at home it was, two sides of the same thing which was very difficult, but Sunday school that that was a man I didn't know other than in the Sunday school so I could relate to him he was very, more like a father I would say. He was consist – he was always kind. And he was playing and he was always very funny very, very fun when we could makes bellow sounds we can, would you say this organ, the harmonium we could pedal . . . I was very curious about musical instruments . . .
>
> (Interview 2, November 2004)

He taught himself to play the harmonium.

> . . . there was one in our basement floor, cellar, which we could play on, it was sort of world outside our parents, just, they didn't point at that organ and say try to play that organ, we just, it was just a world which was accessible to us, it was a door into, a different world . . .
>
> (Interview 3, June 2005)

> . . . there was one in our basement on the ground floor so I think, that was my, way out, from these harsh relatives I started, exploring music as early, as I could . . .
>
> (Interview 2, November 2004)

By

> . . . eight or nine years of age I think, so I think music and teaching, sort of came together in this, in this . . . er . . ., in my ambitions and my ideas of what to, to make out of life.
>
> (Interview 3, June 2005)

When he was eleven-years-old the family moved to the coast and Paul, as recompense for a move he did not wish to make, acquired a piano which he taught himself to play.

> . . . I guess I isolated myself a little with the piano, just sitting with that piano and playing, in the evenings . . .

You said though you sort of isolated yourself by playing the piano, isolated from what?

It was my, it was my time, it was my, it was my space . . . I just play the piano on my own. So that was my time and that was my private room . . . it was my experimental room. It was a sort of freedom I had, so I wasn't very keen on using this for . . . er . . ., for social or for career things, the piano playing was mine.

(Interview 3, June 2005)

. . . I think I just made it just as apart as, [laughs] yeah, lot of music was a thing that you do for yourself, just to answer your feelings. To make up for the hard rest of your life, schooling or whatever . . . So I had a life in music.

(Interview 4, February 2006)

He also played various musical instruments in a variety of social settings.

I got a sense of community there and a sense of belonging and a sense of functioning for someone.

(Interview 3, June 2005)

Compulsory schooling was followed by a period of formal education that was not entirely of his own choosing.

. . . I didn't like, I didn't like school that much, I didn't. I liked some things we could do at school, but schools are more or less teachers and there were so many teachers I didn't, I wasn't inspired by, that, I was quite ambivalent to becoming a teacher myself. Teachers were very different and I, I think I didn't want to become one of them. So why I ended up in teacher training is a story, about a compromise I think, because I guess, I remember, I was very good at art work as well as music. Music was my big hobby, and I wanted to become a musician.

(Interview 3, June 2005)

Since he was about age ten his family had said:

. . . you've got to be a teacher, so I think I was somehow bred. The idea was . . . er . . ., was put into me that I should become a teacher . . . I remember the thoughts were, almost, fed into me that I should become a teacher . . . I think I got a sort of ambition, I think they bred my ambitions of, I started thinking of myself as a teacher maybe.

(Interview 3, June 2005)

> I didn't have particular motivation to become a teacher. They had fed me with the idea when I was ten-years-old. Oh, Paul you, you *have* to be a teacher, you've got to be a teacher, because I was clever at school, should I become a teacher. That was there. That was there for, it's a good enough reason, just if you make good exams, or write, you become a teacher.
>
> (Interview 4, February 2006)

Paul's focus of musician 'drifts'. He also had a notion that he could become an artist and

> I dreamt to go abroad . . . I had a dream, in the college, in the sixth form, to go to Switzerland and study French and music, combine those things, language and music was in my dream . . . That was one dream, to go abroad. So very early I, I, I didn't bind myself to Norway, I think of other places in the world would have been better.
>
> (Interview 3, June 2005)

His parents advised him to become a teacher, albeit a music teacher. Paul's motivation for going to the teacher education college was not for becoming a teacher.

> . . . I did it for music. So I wasn't much interested in pedagogy when I started there I was more interested in playing the baritone . . . So when I was came to teacher training I was very motivated to playing the euphonium again, and I got a proper teacher from the symphony orchestra in Bergen and I was like many, many student teachers at that music line. Music was why we were there. And it was, it was in a fantastic setting just for playing and singing, and there were big choirs, we made recordings in this big choir with 90 students singing and it was, we were taken to, we had excursions to Germany and we were singing with the Berlin, with the Bremen philharmonic orchestra, and it was a world of music. The teaching, the pedagogy [pause] no I think there were only a handful of student teachers there who really came there for, the reason of, we want to become teachers, that's our motivation. So the heart, my heart was in music.
>
> (Interview 3, June 2005)

But then Paul realised:

> . . . when I chose teacher training that wasn't the fulfilment of, my own, so and then slowly I, I had to make up my mind then, I had to make up my mind, would I really become a teacher.
>
> (Interview 3, June 2005)

Having spent some time in the classroom, he

> . . . started to understand, for the first time I understood that well, to be a teacher isn't that bad.
>
> (Interview 3, June 2005)

He became a teacher, remaining in the classroom for only one year before returning to the teacher training college, having been headhunted to lecture there. He was offered a place on a course to become a Master of Music. The course was especially a pedagogic study within music.

> So there my interest in pedagogy was, was boosted you could say. And all the way, all the time since that, since then you had, I had this ambivalence between being a musician and being . . . er . . ., occupied with teaching. And I think that follows most music teachers, that split. The heart is, the heart is split, you have, you have the heart in music and to bind it together with teaching is something you have to do, and you have to renounce on your own, your own ambitions as a musician because teaching takes you away from, from all the time you have practised and played yourself. Instead you help other people to, to become good at playing and singing.
>
> (Interview 3, June 2005)

Although Paul has followed a path of study of music pedagogy/curriculum, culminating in his coming to Britain to complete a PhD, this is not storied as part of a long-standing dream. It does however seem to be a means of threading some meaning into a life that Paul describes, at least at times:

> Hell is on earth, if anywhere. I've been through hell . . .
>
> (Interview 5, December 2006)

Occupational trajectory is one strand of Paul's story; another is his marriage. He met a girl in his home town when he was 19-years-old, shortly before he left home first to complete his military service in the army, and then to go to teacher education college. They were to see little of each other over the next few years although they became engaged. Paul was at college in a distant city, his fiancée remained closer to home, training as a nurse. Paul recalls that in a momentary flash at the wedding ceremony he realised, too late, that he was about to marry the wrong woman. For Paul it became part of a bitter story of his adult life.

... it wasn't a marriage, it was an arrangement. It was an arrangement. It was a script, as you would say, probably, a script. And in a Christian society you never talked about divorce. That was out of the question.

(Interview 5, December 2006)

After 15 years Paul

... one day I said, I think I want a divorce. It was just a matter of saving myself. I was going to the dogs ... I was turning more or less lame, or grey. I was probably, I was probably doing so well keeping up the appearances of what ought to be a happy marriage, because everyone in the church we belonged to thought of this marriage as a good thing. But I, I know with myself that this was because I did all my best. And then I said, I said, I just want a divorce.

(Interview 5, December 2006)

The divorce resulted in Paul breaking away from the religious community that had for so long been a part of his life.

... I started and, to understand that my life was just, in this Christian world, with submission and sticking to the rules.

(Interview 3, June 2005)

It was not only religion that dominated Paul's life, so his story goes. Through the process of therapy, Paul began to recognise that he had been

... sort of foundation for my – a leg for my father ...

(Interview 2, November 2004)

His father had lived his life through Paul and Paul, partly as a result of the strict religious teachings, had

... probably [chuckles] made then to be much more willing to please other people than finding out what was my needs and my will.

(Interview 5, December 2006)

Following his divorce, Paul feels he became a more 'colourful' person, making new friends and taking part in entertainment frowned on by the church. Yet he also talks of his loneliness and of his unhappy years at the teacher education college, only being 'saved' by colleagues encouraging him to become involved in research.

In Norway Paul

> . . . couldn't be myself.
>
> (Interview 2, November 2004)

It is as if

> . . . you have to, pass the sea the seas, to leave something behind if you if you want to, to start a new chapter in your life.
>
> (Interview 2, November 2004)

His move to England presented him with a series of learning challenges.

> The most difficult this maybe, the simplest one just to be myself [long pause] But I'm I'm different, I'm as a Norwegian I am different I don't [pause] when I came when I came here after a while I realised much more, myself than when I was in Norway. That's very hard to explain but, it's more a feeling [long pause] Which didn't mean I couldn't find people here who would understand me or whatever . . . But I think that, [pause] my feeling of being myself I could I could safely be myself . . . just to be myself . . . Just to be myself . . . I am different, I am more myself some, some way. But I think I have changed as well, because when I came over to England that's very hard to explain, . . . er . . ., my allergy, disappeared the same Spring as I came over here I used to have a very hard allergy in the Spring, and I was just waiting for it [laughs] . . . Asthma, asthmatic allergy, voice problems, they didn't appear in, when May came and the birches spring out and everything I didn't have the asthma I didn't have allergy, I didn't have voice problems . . . when I go back to Norway, my asthma comes back . . . And I do, I *do* have a strange phenomenon when I go back to my father, my voice changes. Why does it change when I can, go back to Norway [pause] isn't that me? . . . I can cope much more better with it here.
>
> (Interview 2, November 2004)

Narrative quality

Paul Larsen's narrative is characterised by a high level of narrative intensity. The accounts are lengthy, detailed and elaborate. His written life story, for example, came to 13 pages. In it Paul describes, explains and evaluates. This elaboration is very much in evidence in the subsequent interviews conducted with him in person. It is not possible to 'sense' the amount of rehearsal there is likely to have been of Paul's story from reading the 'journal'; being a written record we have no knowledge of the rehearsal and editing that has taken place in its production. He does however tell us of his response to reading the transcripts of subsequent interviews:

> . . . when I read my story, I was a bit surprised of how much space there was for me, for me being born in the wrong place and wanting to get away. I didn't know, when I read the story, I wasn't quite aware I'd talked so much about it, so I think when you talked to me that was, what I did was just . . . erm . . . reading my thoughts and, as they came, and stuttering a lot, because . . . erm . . . they come from the subconscious, I hadn't told the story before and I tried to imagine myself in, as a little boy, and I was thinking, what was I thinking then? And I tried to get back and think, and get in touch with how I was feeling when I was five.
>
> (Interview 5, December 2006)

Within the transcripts there is evidence that suggest a person who spends much time mulling over his life story in his head along with dreaming of other ways of being. This goes back to his childhood.

> I think I very early on, went beyond the borders that teachers were setting for us. Maybe that's where I get my motivation, or got my motivation from, doing more, just expanding myself in my own, my own thinking and my own fantasy because my fantasy went away with me
>
> (Interview 3, June 2005)

> I think my ambition with schooling wasn't much with academic things, more, it was more like, the personal things, my own motivations. I didn't, I didn't think of starting as becoming a writer or something like that, it wasn't, I like writing and my stories went far above, far above the borders that the schoolteacher set for the writing . . . I went past the topic our teachers gave us and, the task, write about this, write about an experience with this, and when I started writing my associations carried me away, far away from the original experience my teacher was curious about, so I started wandering, so I guess, I guess I, I dreamed a lot, well if you know what I mean, fantasy, dreaming as an inner life, daydreaming more or less. I think I used writing more and more as a daydream. So . . . er . . ., maybe this idea of getting away, getting away from something was, was . . . erm . . . came early into my, not consciousness but into my writing and, I think I used music as well as . . . er . . ., as an escape from, from, restraints and . . . er . . ., rules of behaviour or whatever we were, tied up with, because there were very strict, I would say was rather strict . . .
>
> (Interview 3, June 2005)

[Music] was my daydreaming, first daydreaming was music, I guess, I suppose because I was on my own, and I was happy to be on my own . . .

(Interview 4, February 2006)

But there were also dreams

. . . about flying. Er . . ., literally, literally jumping, jumping down the, the mountainside, that was a dream I had very often. I was walking, down the, the mountainside, then I started jumping, and then I decided not to land on my feet, and I played with this thought in my dreams, it was very real. I had a feeling that I didn't land on my feet, I was just flying, I was just floating away. [sighs] On my own will I decided I wouldn't land, I just floated down there and I enjoyed flying . . . I remember in my dreams I developed this dream, and I could stand in the room and I could just, I could just make a decision, in my dream still, I could make the decision, I took a breath in, I filled my lungs and then I, I ascended from the floor and I was floating in the room and I could just decide to stay up, close to the ceiling, I could, I could sink down but I decided not to touch the floor, so I just, I was just floating. I have had this dream all my life. Just deciding, and it's a fantastic feeling of flying, just of flying. And the feeling in my dreams was, was as if it was real. I actually thought I can fly.

But did you at the time, did you when you when you were young, did you when you were eight or nine when you were having that dream, can you remember?

I had, yes, I remember I had that dream, and I, I thought it was a freedom, I wasn't, I experienced it and it was, it was fantastic, and I experience, I think I experienced this as a, as a freedom, which was worth, made it worth, the strains of reality, because in the night I, in my dreams I escaped from it. So it was a kind of escape.

(Interview 3, June 2005)

Dreaming about other ways of being and other places for being remains an important theme throughout Paul's life. Perhaps the most revealing vignette is when he speaks about his move from Norway.

. . . there are things I miss which makes me think. I'm living in the middle of Norfolk, not a mountain not a river, not, not a sea I miss when I come out to the coast I can just sit there and just, look, and I don't know what it is but, something gives me, a perspective and when I come, down to, Brighton and just look, out and just sit there and see. It brings, well can you say that you are brought back yes maybe I am brought back I lived, close to the sea, and I missed, the row boat, fishing, so of course memories come back, but the distance and time, is the perspective. So what has happened in between, all the things that have happened in between, sort of lines up the perspective I can start talking about myself. Oh that was that that was that time that was that period. Oh that was a hard period, that was a nicer time so I think I start, re-living – can you say re-living? – my life in the head. And I *can* sometimes I'm very good at visualising. So I can bring myself back, to, places, I have been, and even without, shutting closing my eyes but if I close my eyes I'm *there*, and I can see, I can see the picture I can, I can hear the winds I can hear the sea, or some voices are very, easy to recall, some faces are easy to recall so I think I, the exciting thing is, that what was close to me when I was there in Norway, and its, far away now that, that's what I – I had a sentence about the mental, distance . . . and I could hear my father much more. He is much more present now so when you said, he was absent but present, that's mental distance. So, when I visualised, I'm into a situation which I elaborate on. So I think I, well the most exciting thing now is maybe the, the healing side of it I think I can repair the past, by going back, I have an imagination, that things that happen in the past may be repairable. Because when I go, sometimes when I go back, in my head in memory, it keeps me, the feeling the old feeling comes back, when I think of my, serious incidence of claustrophobia for example one time, now later in life I'm, I'm able to recall, the panic I had but now I can repair it . . . when I go back and visualise, I am there again, and I re-live, situations which were, critical or pain – and painful. I can, it's not dangerous for me to, to re-live the pain again, and I just let it be there, and then it disappears, so I think, in that way by re-living my life.

Is it the first time you've felt you could go back there and face the pain?

Yeh, I think so. I think this step has been so drastical so drastic it's so so big, that I have as I said I take more responsibility for my whole life. It's a totalising, experience much more now which, which includes, every small *bit*.

(Interview 2, November 2004)

Visualising, daydreaming, fantasising are common to Paul.

I think I'm a bit, above the surface of the earth, many times. Impossible things. If I were, what if I were in another place of the world, for example. So I think when I read about different parts of the world, the jungle is one part, the desert, stories, I pretend I'm there quite quickly, I think I have got, I don't know from where but I quickly remove myself from the place I'm sitting reading the book or watching the television. I think, I think I pretend I'm there already. So just as these days when I'm, I say daydream, daydreaming, yeah, daydreaming in that sense can be going back, and when I think of episodes and events I've been in, I'm so close to being there the smell of the place comes back, and the feelings, heat, warmth of the sun, smells, sounds, they come back, so I'm so close to being there, if that's daydreaming, I think it is, I think it used to be for me, to be another place. And I don't know why. I don't know why. Yeah, I think it's about wishes to be in another place. I don't think I was born in the right place . . .

(Interview 4, February 2006)

I think music is absolutely a, a way of daydreaming, so . . .

What do you mean?

Yeah. Music is a means, if you go into music, you listen to music, I, [pause] not in the room, you don't need to be in the room any more, just carrying, carrying, to other places.

But what other place was it carrying you to, what, where do you go when you go with music?

[pause] Not other places, necessarily, other times, maybe, the warmer times of the year. Norway is cold. Norway is very cold. And I remember myself when I was freezing. So maybe I just thought about when I was, music is, is energy. And I guess music can warm you up physically, more or less, when you listen to music there is energy coming into you, so maybe this physical side of things with music is just warming, if you just sit there and things start moving, start moving in your head, and your body gets warmed up. If you sit in front of a loudspeaker the energy is just hitting you, isn't it? The ears.

(Interview 4, February 2006)

Paul's life narrative is not only characterised by a high level of narrative intensity and by its analytical and evaluative character. There is also clear evidence of a *plot*, i.e., of an organising principle that guides the selection of events that make up Paul's life narrative and that links these events together and gives them meaning. The plot in Paul's life story seems to be the issue of finding a place – also in a very literal sense – where he can be himself. For Paul the idea of wanting 'a life of your own' is connected to an ongoing search for places and spaces where he can be himself. This means getting 'out of the house' – both the house as a physical environment and geographical location and the house as represented by his relationships with his parents – and is even reflected in his feeling of being born 'in the wrong place.' Music provides Paul with such a space and place. His divorce and break from religion are part of it, as is his move away from Norway, the place where '[I] couldn't be myself.'

There is evidence within the interview data that Paul is aware of this plot. The plot is, in other words, not exclusively an organising principle that is emerging through our analysis of the data. It is also part of Paul's ongoing reflection and narration. It is a crucial and also a difficult part of Paul's reflections. In the final interview we tried to probe this a bit more explicitly by asking him about his search for selfhood.

What were you, and are you, looking for? What are you looking for, if you had to sort of summarise it, when you say, you're looking for this, you're looking, what is it? What's the theme in what you're looking for?

Well, I think, . . . er . . ., I think that's reflected in your questions to me last time. [chuckles] You look for who yourself are, to know yourself and, of course, everyone is looking for love, and what's love?

That's to be, that's to be recognised as the one you are and not being forced into, . . . er . . ., being good enough on someone else's terms. Of course, what's my own terms for being, being me? And that's very hard, that's a very hard question, when you're asked that, who are you? [laughs] That's very difficult. But the theme in this, I think it is just to feel I can say whatever I say without being sanctioned, that I can tell my own thoughts and give my own, tell about what I'm thinking and feeling without being shut down, without ever being stopped. And the Christian culture in, back home was a bit sanctioning, yeah was a bit sanctioning. The difference was music, of course, because no-one sanctioned music, we could just sing. And I think music was a catalyst to, to a reality, . . . er . . ., finding, I think many people find who their self are through, by using music and finding, it's very difficult to say why you like this music or that music. I don't know why I like, I like jazz music, probably because my brother-in-law always, the tunes he was whistling, they were jazz, when I was little he was, my sister was 12 years older than me, so I was just a boy when she married him, I was just 11, and he went around whistling [whistles] always jazz.

But do you think music has worked, I mean, you said there music, finding myself through music, do you think it has worked in, do you feel you have found yourself in that sense?

Well, I'm not a musician who just goes out and holds a concert, for example. I'm not, I don't know if ideas hold me back, for example, the ideas that, I don't have enough technique to, and I don't have, . . . er . . ., I'm not brave enough to become a musician as these who really succeeds and makes a career in music. I never thought about myself making a career in music, but . . .

When you say 'not brave enough', what do you mean?

Standing on a stage and being . . . er . . ., and acting and getting, forgetting yourself, I don't know. You have to step out of yourself, somehow, to be, I always wanted to be a clown, and maybe I can be a clown. I always liked clowns when I was little. I always liked actors as well, so maybe there is a fright there. Why can't I be an actor? And when I was four or five, I always wanted to be a film star or something, I don't know why [chuckles] but many kids might have that wish. So when, how early do you get any, really, idea of who you want to be?

Where are you on that search now of who you want to be?

Now, today?

. . . Mm . . .

Now, I'm in two worlds, I'm in the music world and I'm in the academic world, and it's a very hard, very hard choice, just now when I'm applying for a new studentship again. And someone, I don't know how easy it is to be creative in two worlds, if I, if I, I'm sort of split [chuckles] I'm very split, and how easy it is to be creative in music and at the same time have, doing academic writing and research on these things, it's quite different worlds.

Do you have a sense of, if you were to choose a unified you?

A unified me?

What would it look like, do you know?

Would there be a unified me, I'm, I'm very multiple.

(Interview 6, October 2007)

Efficacy: Learning potential and action potential

The question of what Paul is able to *do* in and through narrative and narration brings us to the issue of efficacy, and thus to questions about the learning potential and the action potential of the life narrative. The first question here is whether Paul has learned anything from the narration of his life. In our view there is abundant evidence that he has. Through the way(s) in which he has analysed his life, has reflected upon it and has constructed a story about his life, he has identified a central theme in his life, namely, the search for a place where he can be himself. The way in which Paul has emplotted his life story is, in this sense, evidence of what he has learned from the reflective construction of his life narrative. What is particular about Paul's case – and this makes his case special and interesting for our understanding of narrative learning – is the fact that although he seems to have identified the search for a place where he can be himself as the major theme in his life, this search – and the narration of this search – is still ongoing. In one respect this is not surprising in that for many the task of achieving a sense of self is a lifelong project. But what is peculiar about Paul's case – particularly compared with some others in the Learning Lives project and others within this particular cluster – is that there is a somewhat circular feeling to all his narration, analysis and reflection. In a sense *Paul continues to look for what he already knows rather than that he uses this knowledge to 'move on.'* In terms of our analytical categories we might say that whereas the learning potential of Paul's narrative and narration seems to be high, the action potential is low. Paul's learning doesn't seem to translate into action.

There may well be psychological explanations for this, but this is neither the focus nor the ambition of our approach. For us the key question is whether we can understand any of this in terms of the particular qualities of Paul's narrative and narration. It is in relation to this that there is a kind of paradox in Paul's narration. On the one hand we would say that Paul is one of the most sophisticated narrators we have interviewed. He seems almost to live 'in narration'. This means that he is constantly rehearsing and recounting his story and seems to live within it – in a real sense it is his primary lifeworld. He also is highly proficient in formal learning milieux. He has completed a PhD late in life and throughout his life has enjoyed work in a wide range of learning genres broadening in spiritual and therapeutic zones of inquiry. Yet this overarching focus for all his searching and learning seems to block rather than promote (other) avenues of action and exploration of selfhood. *There is, we might say, too much narration, reflection and analysis* in Paul's case and it is this that seems to inhibit opportunities to 'move on.' Paul seems imbued with narrativity. After three hours of narrating in interview 5, as the interview is being wound up, Paul comments 'I never tire of this' (Interview 5, December 2006). Constantly, he seems to want to make sense of himself and his world through telling his story. What seems to be the case is that *Paul's narrative activity has become an end in itself, rather than that he is utilising it as a means to draw consequences* that translate into action. With Paul we therefore have an example where the narrative allows for learning. However, this narrative learning does not translate easily into action because there is too much of it and because it seems to have become more an end in itself than a means for action. This seems to suggest that when establishing the action potential of narrative learning, the question is not whether there is narrative learning or not, but about a desirable balance.

8   Eva

Eva's life story goes beyond the simple description of her life. She explains and evaluates, weaving into her story the story of others including aspects of the socio-cultural-political context in which her life has been lived. Like some of the other individuals we have presented in this book, Eva's stories are characterised by a high level of narrative intensity and by ongoing reflection, analysis and evaluation. What makes Eva's case particularly interesting is the way in which her sense of self plays a role in her ongoing storying in such a way that it provides her with a flexibility to engage with new locations and situations in her life. In this regard her case is particularly helpful in exploring the question of flexibility – an issue that connects her narrative and narration to and contrasts it with that of John Peel.

Eva

Eva was born in 1971 in a Transylvanian city in Romania, the daughter of a Catholic Hungarian father and a Jewish Hungarian mother, both musicians. As such she was a member of a repressed minority within Romania and was brought up to observe her parents', especially her father's, participation in counteraction. She was also brought up to have a very strong sense of identity which

> ... mainly originated in the fact that we were, erm we were a minority, and it mainly originated in the political conflictive, repressive situation, and it gave people a very strong sense of identity, ... erm ... because of what you couldn't become. [laughs] So you were who you couldn't become in a way ... you were a Hungarian in Romania, which meant that you couldn't do this and you couldn't do that and you couldn't do the other, ... er ... and that's who you were, you were the person who couldn't [laughs] and that gave you a very strong sense of, of, of ... erm ... of, of ... erm ... something to struggle for ... I think in my early age I was definitely very defined

by, you know, this cultural Hungarian struggle, . . . erm . . . and I was very much part of it.

(Interview 4, May 2006)

Her father, although a musician, encouraged learning across a broad range of interest areas, and especially in science. Although her parents were themselves musicians, they did not initially seek this route as a profession for their daughter. When in pre-school, she declared she wanted to be a violinist, they tried to dissuade her although they ultimately supported her wish.

Both the home and the state were geared to high performance. In both contexts Eva was expected to do well, but she also sought out affirmation from adults regarding her ability. In part, she feels this may have been as a result of a dysfunctional home life. Although Eva portrays her father on the one hand in a very positive light as he encouraged her to be curious about the world around her, on the other hand she tells of his violent alcoholic tendencies that marred her childhood from the age of seven.

Did you always want to excel?

   I think as long as I remember. That's really sad [laughs] it's true. It really is quite sad. But yes, yes, I think so. I think so . . . I think the beginnings were very much . . . because of what was going on at home, . . . erm . . . and I needed to be liked, and I somehow made the connection that excelling will make me liked by adults . . . I liked being liked. . . . Erm . . . and then I worked out that if I'm clever and if I keep being clever and I keep doing, you know, excelling and being the most this and the most that, . . . erm . . . then I'll be liked . . . it was a very particular, it was an intellectual excelling, you know, or excelling in what you do, not excelling as a person, as a, in your qualities, but in what you know and how much of it you know.

(Interview 2, August 2005)

From the age of four Eva wanted to be a musician, not, according to her narrative, because of her familial script but because of a girl who lived in the same 'communist high rise' as Eva:

   . . . little girl age six, started the violin. I was four at the time and I completely idolised her. She was my big friend. And when, you know when a kid starts to play the violin it's not the most pleasant noise [chuckles], and I thought that it was music from heaven and I wanted to do the same. So I was four and I went home and I said I want to do the same as, that girl. I want to play the violin, and my Mum said no way [laughs] absolutely not. And I just said yes I want to play the violin and I had, I have some very nice pictures with . . . erm . . . I had . . . er . . . a sword, I always had you know kind of boys' toys, a plastic sword with . . . erm . . . something that it went into, so I took the sword out of the thing and I started you know, pretending it was a violin and playing with it and saying yes, I'm going to play the violin and not only am I going to play the violin I'm going to play it the other way around, because I'm right-handed, and I couldn't fathom how people could play the violin with their left hand, because it must be very difficult, it looks really difficult, so I'm going to play it with the right hand [laughs] I decided at age four.

(Interview 2, August 2005)

But her parents also provided her with opportunities to begin to dream:

. . . when I was a very little girl, what fired me up was to see someone playing the violin in front of an orchestra. I thought that was absolutely brilliant. That's what I *want* to do. [laughs]
   Right. So you did have that dream.
   Of course, because I was taken to the, again, that was the trajectory that was instilled because my parents took me to concerts. So and put on the records, you know of Yehudi Menuhin playing the Beethoven concerto, I thought that's the most *incredible* thing that I could think of in the world was Menuhin playing the Beethoven concerto. So that was the point of reference. So when I was very, very, *very* little, that's what I wanted to do.

(Interview 5, July 2007)

Although Eva tells of her parents' objections to her realising her dream, nevertheless they ensured she entered music school at the age of six. Eva wanted to excel, intellectually and musically. Her home and school again provided her with the support to do so.

   When she moved to Israel with her mother and brother at the age of 15, she continued to study music. Her new life

. . . was an adventure and that's exactly how it, what it felt like. At first it didn't seem real. It didn't seem like real life. It seemed like everything was different, from, I mentioned I think before, the feeling that, the feeling of freedom, freedom of speech, freedom of thought. That was very, very, very different.

(Interview 2, August 2005)

But there were financial hardships, she was having to learn about new cultures, a new language, and about religion. At the centre of this only books and her violin remained from her 'old world'.

... the violin that came with me, and my identity got very much entangled with, with the violin, with playing the violin because that's who I was. I was someone who came from Romania who played the violin. Erm . . . and I wanted of course to excel, . . . er . . . in that, . . . erm . . . and I understood that I wasn't the best. I was good but I wasn't the best.

(Interview 2, August 2005)

Eva began to have violin lessons with a teacher whose teaching style destroyed her confidence. She began to doubt her ability to succeed in becoming a violinist. At this point, with her sapped confidence and the hardship of life in Israel:

I did have my quasi-religious period, discovering Judaism and what it meant when I was about 16 and 17, and then by the time I was 19 it was, that was over, so, . . . erm . . . I had my little fling with that side, . . . erm . . . and that was important because it was, it was quite a difficult time, I mean I described it as very exciting, . . . erm . . . but you know my Mum was working very, very, very hard and I knew that we had nothing so, you know, the pressure was on to do well, . . . er . . . and, and, the fling with Judaism was something of an outlet, . . . erm . . . so that was, very interesting and, and fascinating and it got me through I think quite, about two quite sticky years.

(Interview 1, July 2005)

Back on track with her music, following a successful and esteem-raising summer camp in America, she no longer had need for religion. It took another teacher and at least

... seven years to persuade me that I could actually become a violinist . . . Even then I wasn't persuaded. [laughs] So it was also self doubt, so I thought, what else could I do if I, and there was nothing that I felt very strongly drawn towards, which also comes from the upbringing, because there was, I mean, the family is so music orientated, that although they have interests in many other things, it was never actually an option to do anything else.

But you know when you doubted whether you could actually be that musician, and it took seven years, you say that it was the other teacher that, to get you to believe that you could, how do you think, though, that you managed to just stay with that, rather than, because some people would have gone, I can't do that and they would have gone off at that point and said, I'm going to do something different.

I think [pause] I think it was mostly fear [chuckles] of giving up. The fear of giving up was bigger than the fear of not making it. And also the, as I said, it's a very commitment-ful engagement, because you have to practise every day and you're supposed to be practising at least three, four hours every day, and I had been practising, you know, two or three hours every day ever since I was, I was very young, and it was a routine, and it was something that was, was very entrenched, that this is who I am and this is what I do. And I was always the one with the violin. Within the family I was the one with the violin because there were no other violinists, different musicians, not with violin. In the school I was the one with the violin, and I saw myself as the one with the violin.

(Interview 5, July 2007)

Eva showed determination and tenacity.

But did you ever, as a child, say, I don't want to do this, I want to go and do something else?

No. No, I was, I always knew this was what I wanted to do, ever since the age of four, when I decided that I wanted to play my violin and my parents said, no way, so, it's typical, you know, little Eva, then especially because they said no, bang [hits table, laughs] I for sure want to play the violin because they said no. It was the same thing all over and over again, something that, you know, I'm very stubborn and very, you know, keeping at it, even if the odds are against it. So that's probably why I stuck with it. And also because, as I say, I was in a, I was in a school system which was, the trajectory was very clear. When I was in music school, I was in music school with all my friends, everybody, that's what everybody did. It was not, I was not alone. It was a very different system than now, for example, if you are in a, in a state school and you play an instrument, you're the odd one out, and you might be picked on or you might be teased or whatever, because you play, and it's a sissy thing to do. But when you're in a specialist music school and everybody plays and everybody wants to be the best in that, and it's quite competitive, then that's what you want to do because of, of the, of the mass, going forward, it's just inertia, it takes you through it. And then when I went to Israel, I, I, and I got to be in the secondary art school, where there were, there were different classes of art, I mean, there were, there were, classical art and ballet and drama and music, and we were the music class. So I saw other kids being interested in other forms of, forms of art, . . . erm . . . but the music class always had the biggest commitment, apart from the ballet class, they also trained very, very hard. And the other thing always seemed to me that that's all very nice that they're doing that, but actually does it take as much of a commitment? I always thought, no, it doesn't really, so that's where we're at and that's what we have to do. Hard work. Good old Eastern European tradition. And I never thought that I should do something else, because I, that was a very good school, it was a very nice school, it was a very good, very good education, so why should I even contemplate doing something else. Erm . . . and when the time came to go to the army and be a musician, being a musician in the army was a way of avoiding normal military service and continue keeping on with your music. Erm . . . and that was another point that it could have diverged, because I could have not got the status, and then maybe I would have done something else, because I couldn't practise for two years. And I know very few people who did that, who didn't get the status and never became musicians, most of them gave it up, so it was something, it became a hobby then, and they did something else. But again, the trajectory took you to the same direction and then it was very normal that, together with that you do the academy, because the academy music had an arrangement with the army, that you could do both, which you couldn't if you studied any other subject, then you had to do your army service and then go to university. But here, there was some kind of arrangement that you could do that, so of course, you would save time because you would be already third year by the time I finished the army and not first, so and that was also, that was something that I always wanted to do, I always wanted to go to music college, and that's it. And then there was the big unknown, you know, what next. And then I became interested in baroque music and I thought, yes, that's what's next. And then it became very much mine. And I think it was at that stage, really, that the script became my script and it wasn't imposed somehow.

(Interview 5, July 2007)

Baroque music was not something she had clearly mapped out for herself as an end 'goal'. The story implies a degree of serendipity.

. . . if I didn't, you know, happen to take a particular course at university and someone, some, a friend of mine didn't drop out of rehearsal and ask me to sub for him in a baroque orchestra, I might not be a baroque musician, and certainly wouldn't be here . . .

Is that how that happened? [laughs]

[laughs] It's complete coincidence. Absolute coincidence. Of course, there were, you know, I can now see that, OK, I was interested in it in a general way before and I was given some tapes to listen and I was always thinking, oh, this is wonderful, and of course it was so different and it was part of the sub, you know, maybe, underground movement that had a huge appeal. But I never thought of actually doing it seriously until

something happened which made me actually do it and then I was all fired up and then I did it.

(Interview 4, May 2006)

She relates the appeal of baroque music to her early life.

And of course because there was something slightly subversive about it, and something not quite mainstream, that was hugely appealing for me. It was just like you know, being involved in the Hungarian side when I was a youth, . . . erm . . . so I got massively involved in that and that was something that is very developed in Europe but unfortunately not so developed in Israel.

(Interview 1, July 2005)

This has become one of Eva's

. . . little crusades. Erm . . . for example, as I said baroque music in Israel is not so, . . . erm . . . is not so, . . . er . . . accepted, not so, not so much liked, . . . erm . . . and I'm, I'm trying for a few years now to go back there and make a little bit of a difference in that, . . . erm . . . and I can see little by little, you know, the, the, people who ten years ago who have thought, you know, come on, don't be so silly, what do you mean, baroque music, . . . erm . . . are now coming and saying oh, actually that sounds really interesting. People who, people who, you know, teachers, instrument teachers, instrument teachers who I knew when I was a student, . . . erm . . . and who then I knew were completely against the whole, the whole idea, . . . erm . . . and now if I do a lecture then you know, some people come and they say actually that was very interesting, and you know, could we listen to a lesson and so on and so forth, so there's a little bit of a difference and that's, that's very nice. So I suppose that's my current little crusade [laughs] which is not at all a social crusade, but [laughs] but it's still something that you know that I can do to prove my point, you know, prove the point.

(Interview 2, August 2005)

Through baroque music she has been able to excel in ways she may not have been able to do in other areas, as a violinist.

Throughout her time at high school and university Eva was changing as a musician. In her early years she always played

. . . very much in tune and with a pretty sound, but it was completely emotionless. Absolutely no expression.

(Interview 2, August 2005)

Through her violin teacher that she went to after the Hungarian violin teacher who had adversely affected her confidence so much, she was taught

> . . . everything I know about, about the violin, and also about, that it's actually to, to express what you feel, which is never something that I thought was part of it. I thought that playing, playing was part of you know overcoming obstacles, you know, there's this technical difficulty there and then you have to get that note, and then you have to come down in that slide and then you have to, you know, the bowing is difficult there, and you know, and overcoming that is the achievement, not actually finding what the piece means and why . . . erm . . . the, the you know, why the composer has written it that way and not some other way. And that was also something that I learned when I was, when I was in Israel and that's one of the biggest differences and it's made a huge difference to who am I today.
>
> *In what way has it made a difference?*
>
> I think it enabled me to, to express some kind of inner, inner voice and enabled me to, to feel that I can express my feelings, not only verbally but through, through music. Erm . . . and that was a, that was a very novel, a novel experience.
>
> (Interview 2, August 2005)

While this was a continuous process

> . . . it happened more and more when I found what I really liked doing which is baroque music actually. Erm . . . because it was something that was definitely mine, and I . . . erm . . ., connected to it more than to the competitive high-powered mainstream music making. Erm . . . and I was definitely becoming more and more aware of the need of the more expressive . . . I finally understood that I actually can become a performer and that I will live up to my own standards if I do, if I do that, because that's something that I feel comfortable in. Whereas beforehand I, I wasn't so sure. Because I wasn't the best I wasn't sure that I would feel so comfortable in doing it. So it was not something that I was a hundred per cent convinced about. I was convinced that I wanted to do music, but I wasn't convinced that playing the violin the way that I did . . . erm . . . was good enough, erm, satisfying enough, etc., etc., etc.
>
> *But that's really fascinating, isn't it, how it changes into something that is far more, there's something else beyond just the technicalities of learning.*
>
> Of course. Of course. Of course. When you, when you start connecting. When you start actually connecting to it, and when you start, when, when the little light goes on [laughs], and you understand that it's actually

part of, part of who you are and part of what you can do with it and it's not just a, the dry, the dry substances of actually acquiring that knowledge or acquiring the skill or acquiring the information, but it's what you do with it that really changes. And it changes who you, well it definitely changed who I am. It changed how, I think how I function, with with people as well . . . I think it made me less, not that I was ever very introverted but it made me more confident in how I relate to people and the fact that I can, . . . erm . . . relate to people in a completely normal everyday way [chuckles] in a way that, that will be understood and will not be mistaken and will not be, that, that would be, you know that would enable dialogue . . . er . . . with another person, and that I'm, it gave me some kind of confidence that I can do it, and I can do it fine, there's no problem.

(Interview 2, August 2005)

Eva's desire to become a baroque musician resulted in her moving from Israel to Britain, where there were more opportunities to succeed. It was a very active decision that Eva took to make the move but

> . . . there was a period of at least ten years when things happened and things came my way, and someone said, well, you should play to so-and-so and then so-and-so said, well, I'd like you to meet, in three years' time, and I did that and then because of that some other things happened. So it all panned out, but without me actually chasing up opportunities, apart from the very initial going and putting myself on the market and going and play-ing to people. And I always just thought, oh, that's nice, that would be nice if that came along, and things evolved from there. Erm . . . but I haven't gone, after kind of the initial bang, it was almost like I was very happy to just float along for a while [chuckles] and go with, go with what comes along.

(Interview 5, July 2007)

But after a time there seemed to be a sense that she could become 'stuck'.

> At some point it has become a stuck line, I mean, it was, it was going very nicely in diverging directions, you know, in this direction and that direction that came along, . . . erm . . . and there were some very exciting things out of that, . . . erm . . . but now it's become a little bit stuck, so now something else is needed, some kind of push is needed . . . I need to do the next step . . . I need to take it to the next level.

(Interview 5, July 2007)

. . . when I started out as a baroque musician, obviously having finished college, I most definitely started as an orchestral musician, as we all do, except the incredibly gifted who straight away go into stardom, . . . erm . . . and I started out like that. But I remember very clearly about 1996 or 1997 thinking, is that all there's ever going to be, is this it now, is this my life now, is it, you know, is this . . . something that, you know, I'm now going to be an orchestral musician in the baroque scene, which is much more exciting than being an orchestral musician in any other scene, so I was thrilled with that and I was thrilled to be playing with, you know, all these world-class ensembles. And I was thinking is that, is that it now, how am I going to make the break to the next level, and then chance came along.

(Interview 5, July 2007)

She was no longer just a

. . . rank and file orchestral player, I was more in a leading position, and from then on came all kinds of spin-offs, erm, of, of things that I'd done, afterwards it all came out from that one event. So in 2000 the game changed and it went to the next level . . . It wasn't actively searched for at that point, no, it came, it kind of came along, and I, again, I seized the chance. But it wasn't something that I went after.

But why do you seize the chance, where there are other people who would just go, that's really nice, but actually, oh I'm quite comfortable here?

Because somehow, yes, because somehow there's this inner conflict about, between the one who still doesn't know, not quite confident if she can do it, and the other one who says, no, come on, you know, you really are better than that, you can do this, so let's see. And I always think that if I don't give it a chance now I'll never know it. So the only way of knowing it is to get yourself out there, and then be prepared for maybe disappointment, which is very difficult to, to deal with. But that's, if you're not in there then you'll never know. If I didn't come here, to England, part of coming to England was to see what I was worth, whether I was worth more than what I could have achieved in the same field in Israel, which was very limited at the time. Erm . . . so I came here to see whether I was good enough to play in very good ensembles, and I thought, you know, it seems to be happening, so obviously that's good enough. So then let's see the next level, am I good enough to do that, OK, now it seems that I'm good enough, and there's still a lot of doubt, a lot of self doubt, you know, am I really good enough, am I really doing the job, it's all self examination going on all the time when you're in that position. I'm not someone who's very, very, very secure and just, you know, goes OK, this is how we're doing it, that's it. I'm one who does, well, this is how I'd like to do it, maybe there's some other possibility, let's see, but let's do it first this way, let's try it this way and then see how it goes.

(Interview 5, July 2007)

Narrative quality

Eva's is another narrative characterised by high narrative intensity. Her accounts are detailed, full of analysis, reflection and interpretation. Eva's life story goes beyond the simple description of her life. She explains and evaluates, weaving into her story the story of others, including aspects of the socio-cultural-political context in which her life has been lived. When Eva was asked to tell her life story she provided four pages of transcript depicting her life and beginning to add some degree of elaboration. She was highly articulate and there is evidence that she is highly reflective. Moreover, being reflective is clearly part of her sense of self. It's not only the way she 'is' – it's also the way in which she understands herself.

> I suppose because I'm the sort of person who always examines what I just did, . . . erm . . . erm . . . I do find myself examining other people's behaviour as well so that I can then draw a conclusion from it, because it is, it is a conscious process, of course it's also an unconscious process . . .
>
> *But the process that you seem to be describing as learning is very much one of observing and reflecting, is that how you'd describe it?*
>
> Yes. I think, I think first you observe and then you reflect because, well I do. I observe and then I reflect and then consciously or unconsciously, maybe more unconsciously, I mould into a certain thing that I think, I perceived as good, as desirable. Erm . . . so, this, process, erm and of course you, I'm sure that I learn . . . erm . . . more unconsciously as well . . .

(Interview 2, August 2005)

Asked about the process of reflection that she has alluded to regarding her musical career, she says:

> I just ponder. I don't, I don't do my pondering in blocks. It comes in little flashes here and there. There is a thought that gets somehow put away and then connects to another thought, I don't know two weeks later and then you recognise something that you've been there already, so then you think umm, that's interesting so what am I going to do about that.

So it's more a kind of ongoing reflection than you'd sit down and think it through.

Yes. It's an ongoing, it's an ongoing thing.

(Interview 5, July 2007)

The ongoing reflection about herself and her life, about her choices and the things that came on her path, work as a plot within Eva's story. She recounts her life and the events in it through the lens of her emerging and ongoing self understanding and self reflection. Doing her *own* thing is obviously very important for her. She feels she needs

> . . . to seize this chance, to seize the, going after something that I really want to do, and to build more on my own things, because I see that that's very important for me. If I do too much just orchestral playing then I get depressed and very moody . . . Because I don't feel that I have my own things to say in that. That's a very different mindset, it's an ant within an ant nest, you might say, because you have your job and you're contributing to the whole, but you're just a little thing in the, you're a very important thing, because if it doesn't work the whole thing collapses, so, but it's a different importance, whereas when you, you know, are up there playing concertos, then *you say* what *you* think about the music, not what someone else thinks about the music.
>
> (Interview 5, July 2007)

For Eva this is 'a constant quest. It goes on. [chuckles] Finding my own voice and what I want to say about the music' (Interview 5, July 2007).

> *But that seems to be, to me listening, that that's the real power and the real drive, is that it's you and your voice.*
>
> Yes.
>
> *And then when you're in this group, it's fine, but actually it has the spin-off of, it can be quite negative for you as well.*
>
> Yes, that's right.
>
> *So how do you deal with the negative?*
>
> The way I dealt with it was that as long as I have something in the pipeline, which I know that is mine and that I can work for, then it's fine, then I can put up with the, then I can accept being just the little, you know, the little.
>
> *Because there's something else out there.*
>
> Because there's something else out there that I can hang onto. It's if, it's when I know that there's nothing for the next three or four months that

I'm preparing for, that's difficult, the difficult part, so I have to make sure that I always have something.

Something of your own.

Lined up. Yes. Yeah.

Again and again Eva personalises the story. She tells of the 'different person' she is in her different roles.

I'm still a musician and I'm still a baroque musician, but I'm being many different people at many different times, so one day I'm being this and the next day I'm being that, and it's *very* different. And sometimes you're a bit, you feel like a little schizophrenic, because you need to assert yourself in a very different way, you need to change the way you behave, because you can't behave as a leader, as a soloist when you're just playing in the orchestra. I mean, some people do, and I know exactly what it looks like. It's horrible. [laughs] They feel that they're big stars. And it, it's a horrible thing, it's not a collegial thing to do so you wouldn't do that. But . . . erm . . . but then when the next day you have, you're a completely different role, and for example, now I'm doing the [production], and I'm not leading one of the orchestras, I'm just leading one of the sections, second violin section of the first orchestra, so it's a fairly minor role to play, and it's fine, it's going very nicely, nicely along and tootles along nicely. But then between two [productions] when there's a week, I'll go off to Iceland to direct something, and I'll be a completely different person. I have to be a completely different person, because I have to, you know, inspire others and get others do, to try out ideas, exciting ideas, etc., etc., so it's, but that's when I, that's when I feel fired up, that's when I feel myself . . . maybe I'm hopeless at it, but it's getting better. It's also learning, a learning curve, since I started a few years ago.

But what is it, do you think, then, that's firing you up? That's the bit that fires me up . . . And I, to be honest, I'm sitting here, and I can see that, because there's something about in your body, in your face, in your eyes, it's going, that's me.

Yes. Yes.

What do you think it is, then, that makes that difference?

Well, there is a, there is a good amount of, probably of control-freakery, because you're much more in control, you're much more in-charge when you're doing that, so I probably live out my controlling, my controlling side much better. . . . Erm . . . but it's also, it's *much* more of a challenge and I'm always up for it, I'm always one for challenges. I thrive when a challenge is thrown in. I'm not very good in just going along, not having a challenge in my [chuckles] and I see, for example, you know, orchestral playing, it is challenging, but it's not challenging in the same way as, as being responsible for the whole thing, for the whole show is [pause] and that challenge gives me a, gives you an incredible high. It's a big, you know, adrenalin rush. So I suppose it's the same, I suppose it's the same as sportsmen competing, when you have that incredible goal and that's where you want to be. You want to be number one, and that's why you do everything. So it's, I don't know why, because I never, that's something that developed much later in my life, I never was like that when I was little. Not in music. I was very good at school, so I was always, you know, the one who piped up, but I wasn't, I wasn't good enough in the violin to be a leader, or to be a director, or to be a, so again, the baroque music gave me a platform where this aspect of the personality could suddenly somehow develop, and it was not, I never thought that this would happen, so it was very, very unexpected, because I didn't think that that was me.

(Interview 5, July 2007)

But for all the narration of the 'unexpected' there is a direction.

. . . if the chance comes up, then I seize it and, and . . .
But it's because it fits with this . . .
It's because of the love of the challenge of it. Because I like being challenged and I do my best if I'm challenged. I don't do very well if I'm just kind of floating along.
But you've already got a direction to your challenge, it's not just any old challenge, is it?
Yes. And the direction, the direction is always to get more, bigger, higher and higher levels of, of self-expression, of authority, of, of being what I call me, in my music-making. Having more and more of a say.

(Interview 5, July 2007)

Although 'autonomy' in this sense plays a crucial role in Eva's narrative and narration, she also puts this into perspective.

I was thinking, certainly myself, I'm sure most people would like to be very autonomous, and very not given to most influences, but then when you take stock, I think actually am I a complete mirror of what I was born to be [laughs] maybe I am. So I was thinking well, in one way my life is, although, if I was asked I would say of course all the choices are my choices, but when I look at it both my parents were musicians, and I am a musician, so that says something. [laughs] Not much deviation, right?

(Interview 5, July 2007)

Efficacy: Learning potential and action potential

Eva not only creates a story which helps to explain and make sense of her life but also creates a narrative and develops narration that provides her with a focus on her sense of self. The process is one of both learning about herself and at the very same time constructing and reconstructing herself. She continuously stories other ways of being and creates or seizes opportunities that allow these strategies to travel the route of their creation. Whilst drawing on scripts available in her socio-cultural spheres she weaves them into a mosaic of her own making. Eva thus presents us with an example of someone with ongoing narrative learning 'in action' and the focus of the learning is very much on the self. We wouldn't want to characterise this mode of narrative learning as 'self-obsessed'. Eva's ongoing reflections on who she is and who she can be clearly have a function in relation to the social events in her life. Within Eva's story there is both stability and instability. Stability may be seen in the form of a continuation of the familial script taking as her life path the career of musician. There was a stability of a kind provided in her childhood through a very structured educational system in Romania, particularly one which provided opportunities for gifted musicians but there was also instability. As a teenager she was uprooted from her home to begin a new life in Israel and whilst this has been storied positively as a new beginning there were clearly hardships connected with this and with her preceding family life in Romania. Through choice she has moved once again to London, and whilst this has provided her with opportunities to develop a musical career it has also been a further stage of uprooting and reestablishment. Through the various transitions in her life Eva has been able to follow a plot built around her identity as a musician. Whilst the form of musicianship has changed in various ways, this has provided the central spine of her story. In other directions she has changed a great deal of her personal mosaic: changing political attitudes, changing her structure of affiliation in music, changing her geographical location. As a person constantly living 'in narration' and highly reflective and analytical she is able to 're-self' in each new incarnation or context. This provides her with flexibility to respond to the new situations and opportunities which confront her, and it is in this way that Eva's case provides important insights for the ways in which and conditions under which narrative learning can 'translate' into action.

9 Russell Jackson

Russell was aged 53 when we first met, and a married man. He identified with the part of the country where he was born and has a strong local accent. He was a willing interviewee, someone with strong views and deep emotions to express, and someone accustomed to self-evaluation. He often referred to himself in humorous, slightly self-deprecating terms. The initial impression one receives of Russell is of someone with a practical orientation and his life story reveals that his skills are grounded in engineering. However, our interviews elicited a complex and at times surprising set of stories, most notably the fact that he spent ten years as a priest. The period covered by the interviews was one of continuing uncertainty and change: Russell was employed in a job that he enjoyed and found meaningful but he would have much preferred to be continuing his vocation as a priest. As the interviews progressed, we were able to trace the uncertainties that Russell confronted in his everyday life as a result of the re-structuring of adult education. At the same time, we documented a deeper transition that was taking place as he adjusted to becoming distanced from his vocation, an issue which was a central theme throughout Russell's narration. Russell himself commented how changes at one level – in his work practices – were 'nested' within a deeper change.

Russell Jackson

Russell was born in 1951, the sixth of seven children in a working-class family that lived on a council estate in a small town in the south-west of England. His father worked in the dockyard and his mother was a housewife. Russell said that he 'always wanted to escape from there . . . out into the big wide world' (Interview 1, November 2004) and an opportunity arose when he passed the eleven plus examination and went to the local grammar school. The experience was not a happy one and Russell described being a victim of bullying:

I was small, I was from [the] working-class, I was rebellious at school . . . in the grammar school, a very snobby grammar school with middle-class parents, middle-class teachers, meant that I stood out. I was, I didn't have the latest bike and I didn't have a new uniform every term or year. I wore my sister's blazer, I remember when she outgrew it, and I was picked on and bullied absolutely dreadfully at school and that's one of the formative things for me.

(Interview 1, November 2004)

Russell left his secondary education at the age of 16 with General Certificate in Education (GCE) 'Ordinary' level qualifications in a number of subjects and Certificate in Secondary Education (CSE) awards in others. He also stated that his grammar school experience left him with a residual bitterness that caused him to detest schools, teachers and everything to do with education for twenty-five years.

It was with some reluctance that Russell followed his father's advice after leaving school and applied for an apprenticeship at a local engineering company. Despite his initial reluctance to apply to the company, he immediately felt comfortable there:

I walked through the green doors of the apprentice school and was hit by the noise and the smell and the sheer engineeringness of that place and I changed direction [laughs] like on the spot.

(Interview 1, November 2004)

This transition was important: not only did it mark the start of paid employment, but in a subsequent interview Russell recalled as his first autonomous career decision the way he ignored his father's cautious advice to apply for a craft apprenticeship (for which there were over 70 available places) and instead applied for a technician apprenticeship (for which there were only six places). Russell recalled his father as somebody who was ambitious for his children but fearful of the risks they might take; he thought his father was surprised by his son's assertiveness.

Russell served his time as an apprentice and achieved a full technological certificate from his local college after five years in 1972. He worked successfully as an engineer for the company for a further six years. During this time he married and the first of his two children, a daughter, was born; Russell's son was born three years later. However, he could see few prospects for further career advancement in his home town and applied for a job hundreds of miles from home:

I ended up in Scotland at twenty-eight, as a short baby-faced Englishman in a hard-nosed quarry of drunken Scots [laughs] and I learned more about handling people and seeing things through in those first six weeks of that job than any other period of my life, really.

(Interview 1, November 2004)

After two years in Scotland he moved to the Midlands where he worked for a succession of engineering companies, including a Finnish-owned company. His career advanced following a trajectory in which he steadily increased his managerial responsibilities – for managing projects, for managing people and for managing money. He found himself undertaking international travel, living in hotels, going to nightclubs, taking business decisions with substantial financial implications. However, from his perspective years later, Russell expressed doubts about the lifestyle:

I'd done lots of things that my family thought were wonderful but actually were boring um and I had this great illusion of being a travelling um up and coming, you know . . . I'd been to nightclubs, three or four nightclubs in cities all over Scandinavia and Europe, and it was all very good stuff um but actually, having done it, you wonder what it's all about.

(Interview 7, December 2006)

Russell was commissioned by the Finnish company to produce a report on its future and recommended that either they invest in a substantial expansion of the business in Britain or cease operations and focus their activities elsewhere. They chose the latter option and Russell was made redundant.

In the mid-1980s came the event that would lead to a major transition in Russell's life, what he described in the interviews as a conversion experience. Although he swore, 'I was damned if I was going to get religion, you know' (Interview 1, November 2004), he was able to pinpoint the occasion when, while undertaking some woodturning at home, he felt his life move in a different direction, the circumstances of an epiphany:

In the garage doing the woodturning and . . . I always get immersed in the woodturning. . . . You reflect there quietly, you're at ease with yourself. You've got a whole pile of things to – you got to sort out.

. . . I'm now turning away happily and minding my own business and I stop the lathe and I'm turning the big pine bowl . . . I'm surrounded with chippings and this bowl is really nice, you know, it's a lovely shape and it's, and it's there. It's in the evening and I've got the light on in the garage shining on this bowl, and I just have an overwhelming sense of a presence with me really. It's really difficult to be, to describe this in rational terms. It's as real to me now as it's always been . . . I had a sense of the real presence of God . . . it's as though something touched me on the shoulder, and I was quite clear in my mind that there was, this was a point of decision for me, that one of the things that God wanted me to do was to become a, . . . er . . . Christian . . . and to join the Church of England, and, and to – that there was a special job.

(Interview 2, December 2004)

So, not only did Russell feel called to become a Christian but also a vocation to become a priest in the Church of England. For someone who came from a family whose religious affiliations were Methodist, a calling to the Church of England was unexpected. Shortly after, Russell was contacted by the engineering company where he had served his apprenticeship and worked at the start of his career and asked to return. The company was running down and eventually closed but, while he worked there, Russell was able to confirm his vocation to become a priest and, in 1988, he and his wife sold their house and used the proceeds to help fund a two year full-time course of study at a theological college.

I had a great, great time. It was a time of great exploration of ideas, of bouncing ideas off other people, debates, ferocious debates sometimes, passionately held discussions.

(Interview 1, November 2004)

After his ordination Russell was appointed to his first curacy back in the southwest of England and this was followed by a decade of working as a priest. Russell spent time in parish work and also undertook a wider diocesan role that involved training others to support children and young people. This was a role he particularly valued and enjoyed. However, in retrospect, Russell judged that he overworked and that his relationship with his wife suffered as a consequence. They undertook marriage guidance but Russell started a relationship with another woman before he had divorced his first wife. A scandal ensued that led to the end of Russell's ministry as a priest.

That is one of the hardest lessons I have ever learned about my own frailty and fallibility, really. I've sat the other side of the table on many occasions helping people who have found themselves in difficult situations . . . To find myself the other side of that coin, with failure and disgrace and everything around, extraordinarily difficult . . . but it was a job I did really well. I just know that about myself and many other people have told me that.

(Interview 1, November 2004)

Thus a further transition occurred, in that Russell still needed to earn a living but he had to adjust to the loss of the role that was central to his identity, his vocation as a priest. He also needed to adjust to changed domestic circumstances after he married his second wife and gained two step-children. Acting on the suggestion of a friend, he managed to secure a fixed term contract with the adult education service to teach computer skills to students who were classified as 'hard to reach' and thus became involved in a new career as an adult tutor. His subject expertise had been acquired during his working life in engineering and through a continuing enthusiasm for exploring new technology as a hobby; however, he held no formal qualification for computer technology.

Russell discovered that he had joined an adult education service where there was great uncertainty about the future. His response to this challenge was to undertake part-time teacher education courses at a local college so that he could ensure his teaching qualification at least met the formal requirements of the service. He also developed a close working relationship with the local principal so that she was aware of his qualities and commitment to adult education.

Russell became a participant in the project after three years of the third phase of his career. While it started with a contract to be an Information and Communication Technologies (ICT) tutor charged with teaching computer skills in remote areas of the community, he steadily developed the significance and scale of his role within adult education. Our interviews traced how Russell adapted to this latest phase of his career but continued to reflect on his vocation to be a priest and on his relationship with the church.

In the second interview, Russell said he had no inclination at all to return to engineering but hoped that at some point it would be possible to return to parish work. He claimed to have significant support for his return among parishioners in his local church. However, he had received an official letter stating that such a return would not be possible in the same diocese. Russell indicated a change in his attitude to being an adult education teacher, that his role as an ICT development tutor was becoming less peripheral and more central to his life:

> . . . where teaching has been until very recently a stopgap measure against the day where I might return to the ministry within the church, I can't see returning to church, so I'm in the process of really coming to terms with the fact and not quite as reluctantly as I might have supposed, that, really the teaching is my career.
>
> (Interview 2, December 2004)

In the third interview, five months later, Russell's professional refocusing as a teacher of adult learners was evident when he elaborated on the ideas and values that informed his practice. He considered himself expert – though unqualified – in his subject area. He was able to develop new courses for new groups of students in unusual locations. He was involved in a pilot foundation degree course in computer science that had been established in partnership with a London university. He spoke of the growing confidence that he had in his work and of the working relationships he had established. However, he was sanguine about the prospects for the service, given the existing funding regime, and feared that: 'Adult Ed I think, will just wither on the vine' (Interview 3, May 2005).

At the start of the next academic year, in September 2005, the fourth interview found Russell still wrestling with the call of the ministry and striving to reconcile it with his occupation as an adult education tutor. In essence, Russell thought he should 'make the most of it' (Interview 4, September 2005). He asserted that he loved teaching and recognised that the role had been a central part of his ministry as a parish priest. He expressed some resentment of what he saw as 'callous and indifferent' treatment from an institution – the church – that uses the language of compassion and forgiveness but, he felt, did not show those qualities to him:

> in the secular world, if I might put it in that way right, I would have been sentenced, I would have served my sentence and I would now be out . . . And in the community which is supposed to be exercising compassion and mercy and forgiveness, that should have been manifested in a practical way, sometime ago.
>
> (Interview 4, September 2005)

It was hardly surprising to find out at the fifth interview, at the end of 2005, that Russell had stopped attending his local church. As his hopes for a return to the ministry faded, so Russell described himself as 'becoming ambitious within the context I find myself in' (Interview 5, December 2005). He was articulate about the professional autonomy in teaching that he saw being eroded by government bureaucracy and the regime of inspection. However, Russell had come to perceive a lack of challenge in his teaching: he was becoming dissatisfied with holding simply a teaching role in adult education and said he was interested in strategic issues and wanted 'to make a difference'.

The sixth interview took place in July 2006, shortly after Russell had been interviewed for two managerial vacancies that had emerged as part of a local re-organisation of adult education. He had been told he was a serious contender for both positions but others had been appointed; Russell was demoralised and disillusioned.

I've come to recognise . . . that I can't continue to operate as a tutor. It will not be good for me . . . I'll stay here because um this is where, for home reasons, I need to stay um but if I were – you know, if I were completely free, I would be long gone.

(Interview 6, July 2006)

The end of his ICT project was drawing closer and he found himself in a shrinking organisation with a new line manager. His response was to meet with senior managers to secure a clearer idea of his prospects within the organisation and to ensure they were aware of his continuing commitment.

At the final interview, it emerged that one of the two individuals appointed to managerial posts the previous summer had decided to leave after a few weeks. Russell was approached and had agreed to accept the vacant post. His responsibilities included such functions as 'improving learning and teaching' and Russell was excited by the potential for becoming involved in more strategic decision-making. He found his new post a congenial one:

My first sort of reaction to that is I'm enormously comfortable in this role. It's like putting on a well-worn coat and just all of a sudden, just go and do the business . . . There are some issues that are going to get addressed and we're going to sort them.

(Interview 7, December 2006)

Asked how he thought things would develop, Russell said he expected the adult education service to change dramatically over the next three years and that it would become a very different organisation from what it had been in the past. He anticipated such change would be painful and saw his role as being supportive of those most affected. He reported that the service had been moved into a different section of the local authority and that a possible scenario for the future would involve much closer work with social services, particularly adult social services.

Russell had formally retired from the Church of England but there continued to be a sense that he had come closest to being what he 'was intended to be' in the days when he was a priest and was working on youth matters for the diocese:

I still find it *really* hard to talk about um the things that I did as a parish priest and as a children's adviser . . . we ran courses for clergy and young people on child protection issues, I did a lot of good in that role . . . I learned lots of things . . . so you see, it's really close to my heart . . . It's been the role um that I felt most truly mine, to what makes me most truly the person that I was intended to be.

(Interview 7, December 2006)

Narrative quality

Russell was a willing interviewee, someone with a wealth of complex stories to tell about his life. His was a first person narrative, a candid account of actions and decisions that he took and of events over which it would seem he had no control (such as his conversion experience). He was able not only to describe key events in his life but able also to elaborate on their significance and meaning for him. It was quickly apparent that reflection on experience was a central feature of Russell's narrative, something he undertook in the interviews and also reported happening at other times and in other places in his life. Russell's stories were thus characterised by a high level of narrative intensity. They were detailed and elaborate and more on the analytical and evaluative than descriptive end of the spectrum. In this regard they were quite similar to the stories told by Christopher and Paul Larsen.

What was particularly distinctive of Russell's stories was the presence of a strong plot within the way in which his narratives were structured and organised. The plot of Russell's life story is his core identity of 'being a priest'. This identity is not about being a priest per se, but is about what Russell was able to do in that particular role, namely, to make a contribution to the well-being of others. It is, therefore, the meaning that 'being a priest' had for Russell, rather than the role itself that matters here. Although it is possible to construct a story of Russell's life in a chronological way, for Russell (or, to be more precise, in the story that Russell constructs about his life) the 'priest-position' works as the centre from which the story is constructed and from which many if not all events in the story get their meaning and are evaluated. With each aspect and dimension of Russell's life story there is always the question – either explicitly posed or more implicitly alluded to – of how it either brought him closer to this core-identity or moved him further away from it. The plot thus not only served as the organising principle in his narrative; at the same time it functioned as an evaluative and justificatory principle. It's the principle he used to evaluate events in his life, and it is the principle through which he justifies what he has done in his life.

Recognition of the central importance of this plot was clearly something that he had a learned from his life – through a complex process of experience, reflection, communication and interaction – and it was something that not only had a significant impact on his life as an 'event' (e.g., the decision to give up his job, sell his house, be trained as a priest); it also had a significant impact on the *perception* of his life, his life narrative, and hence on the way in which he was able to make sense of his life and of himself. Russell's narrative is not simply a descriptive account of a succession of life-events. It has a strong *evaluative* character in that life-events are positioned and evaluated in relation to what is most central and most important for him.

Efficacy: Learning potential and action potential

When we ask what kind of opportunities for learning and action Russell's narratives provided, we can conclude that *the plot was a major device for Russell's narrative learning*. Unlike with Christopher, whose narrative learning was more a process of ongoing emplotment and re-emplotment, the plot that functioned in Russell's story remained relatively stable, although, as we have said, the recognition of the importance of his core-identity was itself the outcome of a learning process, rather than that it was something he started out with in his life. Whereas Christopher developed an idea of a sense of trajectory fairly early on in his life and, so we might say, spent the rest of his life in search of the trajectory, with Russell the sense of direction emerged at some point in his life – and in Russell's narrative it's presented as a conversion experience – and from then on became his trajectory and a reference point for reflection.

It is clear from Russell's narratives that reflection played an important role in how he lived his life, although he did comment that taking part in the project had provided him with significant opportunities for more and further reflection. When, in the final interview, he was asked to evaluate the experience of taking part in the project, he answered:

> I think it's been an important one and one which is immensely personal. It's been an opportunity to reflect on my own life . . . in ways which I do anyway but, you know, within a formal context . . . [A]ctually trying to work out what it is that you want to say in a coherent way when you're being faced with personal and piercing questions then that's a really useful reflective tool that has been of great value to me . . . The other thing that's happened is reading the transcripts and the transcripts have been hugely moving for me on occasion to read. Somehow it definitely makes you step aside from the talking and then to go back and read this, one is both embarrassed and I found, touched by the story that [laughs] one is reading and that may sound sort of selfish or sort of self sort of narcissus-like, but that has been a new experience for me . . . Unless you are asked the question, unless you're pressed, unless you're asked to explain that, what is just internal, what is just accepted within yourself as being the way the world is, is not brought out, you know?
>
> (Interview 7, December 2006)

There are three important facets to this response that give us insight into the nature of Russell's reflections: first is that he confirms a disposition to be reflective and that the interviews gave him a formal context within which reflection could take place; second is that this formal context required him to identify and articulate responses in a way that private reflection would probably not have done; and the third concerns the transcripts, that he found reading the transcripts to be both embarrassing yet 'hugely moving' and this was an unaccustomed form of reflection for him. The availability of such a reflective space showed how even someone as experienced and sophisticated in reflection as Russell was capable of achieving new insights from narrative processes.

In considering occasions when narration or story-making might lead to learning, we noted that Russell's stories gave prominence to workplace relationships, when there were opportunities for exchanging stories with colleagues or friends who have been important at different times in his career: there was a diocesan colleague with whom he worked on matters affecting children and young people; there was a friend in the education service who suggested that Russell consider employment as a teacher of adults; more recently there were adult education managers who had come to value Russell's experience and the discourse that this enabled. Russell was aware of the way he used reflective spaces such as the opportunities given by colleagues. The project interviews gave even greater opportunities for reflection:

> [T]hings do affect me, very deeply, very profoundly and um those long pauses [*marked in the interview transcripts*] are partially to try and work out myself what I, how I can express what I feel and partially to, for me to um keep control of um myself.
>
> (Interview 4, September 2005)

In contrast, Russell commented on a relationship in which it seemed there had been little exchange: he had spent twenty-six years with his first wife, whom he described as an intelligent and capable woman, and yet he said he did not know very much more about her at the end than he did at the beginning of their marriage. He observed:

> I didn't *know* her story because she never told me her story, in that sense. I never *knew* her interpretation of the story that we shared.
>
> (Interview 7, December 2006)

With his capacity for reflection and evaluation and with his use of opportunities that have arisen over the years to develop his narrative, Russell has managed to overcome some of the 'scripted' stories that might have constrained the life possibilities of someone with his socio-economic background. His story of passing the eleven plus examination finds resonance in many other stories of 'bright' working-class boys going to grammar school. However, Russell's capacity for reflection seems to have given him a means to revision his life substantially on later occasions. In Russell's case there appears to be a close correlation between his capacity for narrative learning and the possibility of continuing to reconstruct his life.

With Russell we have an example of someone with a life narrative more than a life story, most notably because the life is storied around a clear plot. The plot is articulated in terms of a core identity and core understanding of the self, and at the same time reveals something of what Russell has learned from his life. The plot is not a construction from the outside; Russell is clearly aware of the central significance of the priest identity in his life and storying his life has been an important vehicle for him to make sense of his life and the role of this identity in it. His sense of identity has had an impact on how he has led and is continuing to lead his life; it has also helped him to live with the consequences of the decisions he made.

The narrative we can construct from the interviews suggests that Russell's stories and story-making fulfil two functions. The first is that *storying is a tool for reflection*: life stories allowed Russell to 'objectify' his life, to make it into an object of reflection so that a different understanding of life can be achieved and the process helps make conspicuous the values that are important. The second is that *storying has an integrative role*: it is possible to achieve synthesis of different aspects of experience, the integration of different forms of learning over time, through the process of making stories. Russell's life stories show how there are identifiable 'things' that he learned *for* his life, such as the knowledge that enabled him to follow his career. However, such identifiable learning is inseparable from the understanding that Russell has developed over the years about himself, about his character and dispositions, and how that self relates to others in his family, in his workplace and in his social networks.

Russell's stories of formal education and training reveal some of the information, skills and competencies that qualified him to earn a living and gave him access to different careers. Associated with each of the three stages of Russell's career was a period of formal education and training: the apprentice school before his engineering career; theological college before his career as a priest; teacher education courses in a local college while he became an adult education tutor. Each of those periods of formal education offered immersion in the culture of a different community and offered opportunities for interaction and communication with others. Russell seems to have used them as spaces for reflection on his life.

Having secured entry to these different career fields, Russell's progress within them depended on other forms of learning. His career trajectory within engineering moved steadily away from engineering per se to more managerial responsibilities and this occurred largely without formal training. The stories about his church career again suggested he undertook different inquiry and study – within formal courses and in informal and non-formal settings – that enabled Russell to sustain and diversify his career. Within adult education, our interviews monitored the way Russell's aspirations evolved and refocused, how his ideas of the person he might be in this field became more ambitious. Learning achieved within formal education and training that has defined or identifiable outcomes shifts within the narrative to become forms of learning that have significance for the maintenance and development of the self.

The nature of Russell's learning from life stories is even more evident when we consider the values that frame his approach to life. Russell's stories reveal that he has a normative and ethical stance from which he evaluates his experiences. His values are often traceable to experiences within formal education though they were rarely part of the formal curriculum. In his stories of grammar school life and his comments about bullying, for example, we find some of the origins of Russell's opposition to injustice. He recognises this school experience as 'one of the formative things for me' and asserted that 'I will not be bullied, I will not be intimidated, I will not be forced into anything that I don't wish to be' (Interview 1, November 2004). In stories of later events, such as dealing with the problems of parishioners when he was a priest, Russell demonstrates a continuing determination to take a stand against perceived injustice. The scandal occasioned by the loss of his career as a priest appears to have enhanced the empathy that Russell has with people who are disadvantaged or who have experienced disasters.

In the final interview we heard Russell's thoughts about coping with the challenges of his latest post in adult education. His resources were a lifetime experience of working, from the age of sixteen to his fifties. He was able to identify experiences and resources on which he could draw when confronting current problems: he spoke of the counselling skills he developed in different courses and the importance of his private reading as threads that became intertwined with the accumulated experience of being a parish priest. They give him the confidence and self-assurance needed to adapt to new circumstances.

Russell's case thus not only shows how there was ongoing learning from life through reflection and narration; it also makes clear how in his case this learning 'translated' into action. Russell's insights into what mattered most to him – a particular way of being for others – provided him with criteria, so we might say, to make decisions at important transition points in his life. This is not to suggest that Russell was in total control of his life – on the contrary, his life story is full of events that happen to Russell rather than that he actively chooses them. Yet it is the response to such events that is significant in understanding the action potential of Russell's narrative learning – a learning that never became an end in itself, as in the case of Paul Larsen, but always remained a means for living his life. On Russell's own account story-telling did indeed play an important role in all this.

> I'm not well qualified. I'm not, you know, hugely intelligent or all those really worthwhile things, I've just got a story. And the story informs who I am and the story makes me who I am and out of that I have an ability and a confidence and the ability to deal with people in their stories.
>
> (Interview 7, December 2006)

10 Towards a theory of narrative learning

In the foregoing chapters we have presented and reflected upon the stories from eight individuals who took part in the Learning Lives project. Our reason for selecting these eight was not that the other participants in the project had nothing interesting to say, and also not that only these eight provided evidence of narrative learning. The main reason for our selection is that the stories of these eight individuals allow us to explore those differences in narrative quality and in learning potential and action potential that we identified as important on the basis of our analysis of a much larger number of cases. The stories of John Peel, Marie Tuck, Maggie Holman, Diogenes, Christopher, Paul Larsen, Eva and Russell Jackson are, in this sense, exemplary for the variety of aspects and dimensions that we see as crucial for understanding and theorising narrative learning.

As we begin to theorise the different aspects and dimensions of narrative learning, we wish to warn against any assumption of a hierarchy of esteem or well-being related to the distinctions we introduce. The examples of John Peel and Paul Larsen show elegantly that, just as low narrative intensity and an absence of any explicit narrative learning can be a clear route to well-being and fulfilment, so high narrative intensity and elaborate analysis can be a 'narrative maze' imprisoning the individual in learning without empowerment. So whilst the distinctions we have made and will reiterate in this chapter allow us to characterise important elements and dimensions of narrative and narration, this does not in any sense define a capacity for fulfilment or well-being. At root our understanding of different aspects and dimensions of narrative learning warns against any absolutist notions of social or psychological determinism. This is not – it should be noted – to argue that future work on narrative learning will not elucidate patterns related to, for example, class, gender and ethnicity, to regional, cultural and historical variation, or to personal aspects, factors and dimensions. Our focus on narrative and narration does, however, offer an insight into the complex variations which underpin, and indeed sometimes override, such categories and stereotypes.

Richard Hoggart has written autobiographically about his own impulse, his own 'push for meaning outside the day to day' (1958: 89), which he sees as a capacity to theorise and elaborate alternative imagined futures. His work refers back to the ossified class structures of his youth when working class solidarities were appreciable and appreciated. In his world descriptive narration was viewed as the predominant working-class modality, although his own autobiography warns against over generalisation. Hoggart writes:

> Almost all working class people have been used to living as subject to merely successive events. If the assault has a pattern it is that of birth and growth and death, it is that of seasons and main dates of the year and of weekly wage packet. Working class life has long been dominated by the thisness of things and events and people; an unordered thisness. . . . What almost all working class life – almost all levels of life – avoids, or, better, is unaware of, is intellectual pattern-making, generalised across and about habits in space and time, and so of gathering such generalisations together and hazarding judgements. To generalise about them is strange and can be disconcerting.
>
> (ibid.: 213–14)

Joe Bageant has produced a similar insider account of white working-class folk knowledge in the USA. He says:

> My people don't cite real facts, they recite what they have absorbed from the atmosphere. Theirs is an intellectual life consisting of things that sound right, a blend of modern folk wisdom, cliché, talk radio and Christian radio babble.
>
> (Bageant 2007: 9)

In scrutinising our data, we have not specifically attributed narrative description collectively or individually to working-class participants. As a characterisation of descriptive narratives Hoggart and Bageant capture some of what we have found about the learning potential of such narratives, but we do not wish to discern a monolithic pattern of social class attribution. Descriptive narratives can work with the grain of social scripting and in those cases such narratives tend not to move systematically beyond such scripting. But as we have seen, description is a narrative form that works through personal variation, for whilst some accept their initial given script, others move between scripts. Fluidity, social mobility, social movement and flexibility of response are thereby also found in descriptive narratives. Hence forms of narrativity whilst they may be socially patterned are always personally inscribed. To understand the social then, we also must always pursue the personal and must take personal stories seriously in their own terms and not just as the expression of something underlying or overarching (see also Biesta 2010). This, above all, is why we have provided personal portrayals as the starting point for any conceptualisation of narrative learning.

Narrative quality, narrative learning, and the question of action

Narrative learning can be evidenced in the substance of the narrative but also in the act of narration. Narrative learning, as we have said in the introduction chapter, is therefore not solely learning *from the narrative*; it is also the learning that goes on *in the act of narration* and in the ongoing construction of a life story. Within the cases we have presented in this book there are already important differences in relation to this. Some stories are short, descriptive, and, in a sense, finished. Other stories are more elaborate and contain elements of analysis and evaluation. Whereas the first kind of stories give the impression that they are more scripted and less the result of learning – the working and reworking the story of one's life in response to experiences and on the basis of reflections – the second kind of stories seem to provide evidence of narrative learning, that is of learning done through the construction and reconstruction of the story of one's life. But such stories can have a finished quality as well. They are more the products of past narrative learning than that they are evidence of ongoing narrative learning. This is what, in our view, unites the case of John Peel with that of Diogenes. Although the stories they have to tell about their lives are significantly different in narrative quality – in terms of intensity, description/analysis and the presence of a plot – the stories themselves are more closed than open; they have a more finished quality. Nonetheless, as we have seen, these stories are important 'reference points' for their achievement of a degree of agency in their lives – they are not, in other words, without action potential. John Peel helps us to see how a 'finished' life story can be very functional if it 'fits' with the context, but loses its efficacy when circumstances begin to change and the fit is no longer there. With Diogenes it is, perhaps, more the strength of the values and convictions that were central in his life story that allowed him to operate effectively under changing circumstances, albeit that new circumstances remained 'measured' against a set of values that was developed in the past. Closed life stories, to put it differently, are therefore not without action potential although the relative inflexibility of such stories makes their utility as a tool to engage with changing circumstances sometimes more limited. In this sense we can think of our narrative resources as a kind of 'narrative capital' (Goodson 2006) – the narrative 'repertoire' that can assist us in navigating change and transition in our lives.

But as we have seen, the narrative resources that people have available differ widely in their characteristics – their narrative quality – and in their efficacy. It is here that we wish to remind the reader of two important findings from our analysis. The first is that the presence of an elaborate, analytical and emplotted narrative is not, in itself, evidence of *ongoing* learning. It is here that the distinction between the narrative as the outcome of learning and the narration as a process of ongoing learning is important in theorising narrative learning – and we can characterise this as a distinction between more 'closed' and more 'open' narratives. But what our cases also show is that more 'open' narratives – narratives 'under construction,' so to say, narratives where there appears to be ongoing narrative learning – are not in themselves a guarantee for 'translation' into action. This is how we have suggested to read Paul Larsen's case, that is, as an example of narrative learning where the learning, the ongoing development of narrative resources, seems to have become more an end in itself rather than a means towards other ends. There is, as we have put it, too much narrative learning going on which, in a sense, gets in the way of action. Ongoing narrative learning seems to have become the centre of gravity of Paul's life. And although this provides him with significant opportunities for reflection, action comes, by a long distance, as a secondary concern – and in some respects it does not come at all. While Socrates may have asserted that the unexamined life is not worth living, Paul Larsen's case reminds us that the opposite is sometimes more true, i.e., that the unlived life is perhaps not worth examining (Biesta 2002).

On the basis of our data it is difficult to say why some people's narratives are more closed and why others' are more open. Similarly it is difficult to say why in some cases narrative learning 'translates' into action, and in other cases not. There is, however, one important pattern emerging from our data that seems to suggest that in those cases where the self is part of what the ongoing narration is about, the narrative has a tendency to remain more open – which, in some cases, seems to impact positively on the efficacy of the storying, that is, on the action potential of narrative learning. The question of self connects our analysis with issues concerning identity and agency. It is important to keep those two terms together in understanding the self because a discourse solely in terms of identity runs the risk of moving the question of narrative learning too much towards self-referential if not self-obsessed forms of narration and learning.

Our cases provide ample evidence of reflection on, storying about and re-storying of the self. We saw this, for example, in the case of Christopher's personally crafted narrative and his ongoing narration. There we argued that the personal element of his narrative and narration did not so much lie in some kind of 'carte blanche' but more in a systematic 'bricolage' by which a personal mosaic is created of many different, socially available scripts. In Christopher's case this personally crafted creation provides a vocational pathway and livelihood throughout his life and an existential agenda. A similar kind of 'harmonisation' of learning, identity and agency construction can be found in Eva's case where we observed that Eva not only creates a story which helped her to make sense of her life – which shows how her sense of self is the central element in the ongoing emplotment of the life story – but also creates a narrative and develops narration that provides her with a focus for identity development that is not just self-referential but has important action potential. Our discussion of Russell Jackson's case provides further clarification of these elements of narrative learning in relation to self, identity and agency. As we wrote in Chapter 9:

> The narrative we can construct from the interviews suggests that Russell's stories and story-making fulfil two functions. The first is that *storying is a tool for reflection*: life stories allowed Russell to 'objectify' his life, to make it into an object of reflection so that a different understanding of life can be achieved and the process helps make conspicuous the values that are important. The second is that *storying has an integrative role*: it is possible to achieve synthesis of different aspects of experience, the integration of different forms of learning over time, through the process of making stories. Russell's life stories show how there are identifiable 'things' that he learned *for* his life, such as the knowledge that enabled him to follow his career. However, such identifiable learning is inseparable from the understanding that Russell has developed over the years about himself, about his character and dispositions, and how that self relates to others in his family, in his workplace and in his social networks.

Whilst in all of these cases learning, agency and identity constructions are to a degree harmonised, in each case the balance is different and judgements about efficacy vary accordingly. The delicate equation of how life narratives are employed and how narration is processed depends on the balance of learning, identity and agency. We saw in Chapter 2 how John Peel developed his identity around a well-established role as a farmer. His life story was concentrated within this farming milieu. As a result of accepting and following the farming script he was unpractised in narrative learning and the process of narration – commenting at one stage, whilst recounting his life story, that it seemed a 'false' conversation. When the context of farming changed this left John in a very unfamiliar situation, for in a sense his whole life world was changed by external forces beyond his control. His birthright script was redundant but he was unpractised in script development since he was primarily used to following the script he had, a script that served him well for most of his life.

In Chapter 3 we saw Marie Tuck moving, during the course of the interviews, from a descriptive towards a more analytical and evaluative mode of narration. One of the fascinations of longitudinal study is the capacity to register these 'life-course' changes and, particularly in Marie's case, the accompanying changes in narration and narrative learning. Her celebration of agency and identity transition is very deeply felt. As she put it: 'I'm a single mother of two that can stand on her own two feet, doesn't need you or anybody else. Don't want you or anybody else ... And I just felt so bloody good, I tell ya, and I still do' (Marie Tuck, Interview 7, February 2007).

Paul Larsen remains an important exception to all this because whilst there is ongoing narration that is clearly focused on the self – and in this regard the quality and content of his narration is similar to that of Christopher, Eva, Russell Jackson and, eventually, Marie Tuck – his case shows that ongoing 'identity work' in and through narrative learning is not, in itself, a guarantee for a 'translation' into action. As we mentioned before, our cases show that it is more likely that open narration of this kind 'translates' into action, but the efficacy of such forms of narrative learning remains without any guarantees.

Maggie Holman's case provides us with another important reminder about some of the limitations of narrative learning. When we concluded, discussing her case, that there is no real evidence that for Maggie narration functions as a site for learning, we were not trying to suggest that Maggie was not learning, but that she was not using narrative and narration – which we basically depicted as temporal rather than as spatial devices – to learn from her life and the storying of her life. Maggie's case thus helps us to see that narration is not a natural necessity, but a particular 'tool' that some people can use and find useful. But the 'tool' itself is not one that everyone has available or that works for everyone. It can work for those with narrative cognition, but Maggie's case shows that it has limited or no use for those with non-narrative forms of cognition – or, as in Maggie's case, a form of cognition that we referred to as 'pictorial'. The more important question, perhaps, is why nowadays so many people feel relatively comfortable with narrative and narration, with life story and life history. Perhaps the pervasiveness of narrative and narration in modern life is something that should worry us and needs further investigation, rather that it should simply be accepted. Zygmunt Bauman, in his book *Liquid Modernity* (2000), has argued, for example, that the erosion of the public sphere not only happens through neo-liberal incursions from the side of the market, but also through incursions from the private sphere (e.g., through the growth of reality television and other modes of confessional popular culture) that amounts to a celebration of the personal without asking more difficult questions about the processes through which personal issues can be transformed into public issues that have political rather than just personal significance.

The complex ecology of narrative learning

Our case studies leave us with a complex ecology of narratives and narration as would be expected in such an intricate and intimate aspect of human activity. Some of the distinctions that emerge from our studies are important in theorising narrative learning.

The key distinction that emerges is that between the use of life narratives as tools for learning, agency and identity construction and the ongoing process of narration itself as a site for learning. What all our cases show, but is particularly highlighted by Maggie and Diogenes, albeit for different reasons, is that the first category, employment of life narratives as tools can exist in an intensive and active manner without the presence of ongoing and pervasive narration activity. It would seem from our studies that while most people do recount life stories when interviewed, not everybody works with narration as an ongoing, internal conversation or external accounting mechanism. Narrative learning, then, appears to take place in two ways. First, learning can take place by the employment of life narratives as tools for facilitating learning strategies. Second, learning can take place at the site of 'narration' itself, through the ongoing internal conversation and external accounts that are undertaken as a genuinely lifelong process. From this angle, narrative learning is maximal when in evidence as a tool in the form of a life narrative and as the site of ongoing narration. There is however a complex ecology to narrative learning. As we have shown, not everybody learns in this way and there are considerable personal variations.

Our case studies indicate that the maximal capacity for narrative learning is reached when life narratives as tools and narration as ongoing activity are active and in a productive balance. In these cases – Christopher, Eva, Russell Jackson – the learning potential and action potential are substantially explored. We might see this as a type of *open* narrative learning where all the channels for learning are open. The key issue in theorising narrative learning is the issue of balance between the various aspects and dimensions. As we have said before, the case of Paul is significant in that whilst the narrative learning is highly intense and the learning potential considerable, the action potential is not fully explored. Likewise in the case of John Peel we see the development of a life story based on established socially recognised scripts but with virtually no ongoing narration. This is a *closed* form of narrative learning with virtually no channel between the narrative and narration. As a result the flexibility of response to new life experiences and events is diminished. Diogenes also represents a closed model where the narrative is a finished product, a final script almost, with no ongoing narration or modification, although in his case it is the 'strength' of the convictions that stem from his narrative learning that allow him to operate in different contexts and under different circumstances, but at the risk of becoming cynical about those situations. In Marie Tuck's case we see in fascinating detail the transition from closed narrative learning to open narrative learning. The balance of narrative as static tool through to ongoing narration and narrative reformulation changes dramatically. In this case we see the move to narrative learning in action. There the culminating process is open, flexible, a work in progress.

At its best narrative learning provides a suitable model for learning through the life-course, for the development of a nuanced and flexible response to the challenges and changes which life brings. Strategies to facilitate narrative learning are currently unexplored and hence underdeveloped. To explore its potential will require an urgent and overdue examination for new learning resources and new learning environments. For all those interested in education as a route to self development and social purpose narrative learning would seem to offer a promising gateway.

Coda

Whilst we have not interrogated the social pattern of narrative learning we are aware of the different social contexts in which such learning is embedded. Like other forms of learning people are differentially resourced and located with regard to narrative learning. What we have shown is that narrative learning goes on in the lives of people, is significant for them, and can be an important vehicle for personal agency and identity construction. In this regard we not only present a new way to understand learning, but through this are able to identify learning processes that are highly significant for individuals and the ways they act in society. Narrative learning is a way to understand learning that instead of dealing with the acquisition of externally prescribed content (such as a defined curriculum) explores the learning which is involved in the construction and ongoing maintenance of stories about one's life. Our case studies indicate that a substantial number of people spend time rehearsing and recounting their life story in a way that is a highly significant part of their actions and agency. Narratives and narration reveal themselves as potentially important tools and sites of learning with substantial implications for subsequent action. Since people themselves are engaged in the construction of the narrative there is not the problem that so often troubles learning in relation to externally prescribed curricula, i.e., that of ensuring engagement. Narrative learning seeks to shift the focus to an area where from the beginning there is engagement and motivation in place.

The Learning Lives project started trying to understand learning from a different position to that which is normally taken. We started by asking people about their life histories and began to focus down on the main learning incidents in their life. Significantly for many people this did not involve externally mandated curriculum but grew from internally generated narrative activity. Often people are engaged in what we have called 'an interior conversation' where they work out their position on things; define courses of action; create stories and life missions. We take this as an important part of a person's map of learning and way of understanding of how they act in the world. There is, however, a danger involved in making such processes – which first and foremost are personal processes that have meaning for individuals in the ways in which they make sense of self and life – visible. The danger is that what starts out as something that is personally significant becomes colonised by educational, economic and social systems. While in this book we have tried to indicate how learning through narrative and narration 'works' and how it can be significant for some individuals in the ways in which they live their lives, we have not only emphasised that narrative learning is neither a necessary nor a sufficient condition for leading a happy and rewarding life; we also wish to emphasise that the very thing that should not happen on the basis of our exploration of narrative learning is to demand from individuals – either within school contexts or as so-called 'lifelong learners' – that they engage in narrative learning or become 'narrative learners'. Narrative learning is a highly personal form of learning. It is one that people can decide to engage in more explicitly or not, but it is not something that can or should be demanded from anyone, nor should it be seen as a panacea for the problems that educational institutions are currently faced with. Narrative learning belongs to the domain in which, as Carl Rogers (1969) has put it, individuals have a freedom to learn. Narrative learning provides one avenue through which people can pursue this freedom to learn in a rigorous and vigorous manner throughout their life-course.

Bibliography

Alheit, P. (1995) 'Biographical learning: theoretical outline, challenges and contradictions of a new approach in adult education', in P. Alheit, A. Bron-Wojciechowska, E. Brugger and P. Dominicé (eds) *The Biographical Approach in European Adult Education*, Wien, Verband Wiener Volksbildung, 64, 57–64.

—— (2005) 'Stories and structures: an essay on historical times, narratives and their hidden impact on adult learning', *Studies in the Education of Adults*, 37, 2: 201–12.

Antikainen, A., Houtsonen, J., Kauppila, J. and Huotelon, H. (1996) *Living in a Learning Society*, London: Falmer Press.

Bageant, J. (2007) *Deer Hunting with Jesus: dispatches from America's class war*, South Africa: ANZ.

Bauman, Z. (2000) *Liquid Modernity*, Oxford: Polity Press.

Biesta, G.J. (2002) '*Bildung* and modernity: the future of *Bildung* in a world of difference', *Studies in Philosophy and Education*, 21, 4/5: 343–51.

—— (2006) *Beyond Learning: democratic education for a human future*, Boulder, CO: Paradigm Publishers.

—— (2010) 'A new "logic" of emancipation: the methodology of Jacques Ranciere', *Educational Theory*, 60, 1: 39–59.

Biesta, G.J. and Tedder, M. (2006) *How is agency possible? Towards an ecological understanding of agency-as-achievement*, Learning Lives working paper 5, Exeter: The Learning Lives project.

—— (2007) 'Agency and learning in the lifecourse: towards an ecological perspective', *Studies in the Education of Adults*, 39, 2: 132–49.

Biesta, G.J.J., Goodson, I.F., Tedder, M. and Adair, N. (2008) *Learning from life: the role of narrative*, Learning Lives summative working paper, University of Stirling: The Learning Lives project.

Booker, C. (2004) *The Seven Basic Plots: why we tell stories*, London: Continuum.

Brooks, P. (1984) *Reading for the Plot: design and intention in narrative*, Oxford: Clarendon.

Bruner, J. (1986) *Actual Minds, Possible Worlds*, Cambridge, MA: Harvard University Press.

Bruner, Jerome S. (1990) *Acts of Meaning (the Jerusalem-Harvard Lectures)*, Cambridge, MA: Harvard University Press.

Burke, K. (1945) *A Grammar of Motives*, Berkeley, CA: University of California Press.

Chamberlayne, P., Bornat, J. and Wengraf, T. (eds) (2000) *The Turn to Biographical Methods in Social Science*, London: Routledge.

Clandinin, D. and Connelly, F. (1991) 'Narrative and story in research and practice', in D. Schon (ed.) *The Reflective Turn: case studies in and on educational practice*, New York: Teachers College Press.

Connelly, F. and Clandinin, F. (1990) 'Stories of experience and narrative enquiry', *Education Researcher*, 19, 5.

Czarniawska, B. (2004) *Narratives in Social Science Research*, London: SAGE.

Dominicé, P. (2000) *Learning from Our Lives: using educational biographies with adults*, San Francisco, CA: Jossey-Bass.

Ecclestone, K., Biesta, G.J.J. and Hughes, M. (eds) (2009) *Transitions and Learning Through the Lifecourse*, London: Routledge.

Garfinkel, H. (1967) *Studies in Ethnomethodology*, Englewood Cliffs, NJ: Prentice Hall.

—— (2002) *Ethnomethodology's Program: working out Durkheim's aphorism*, Lanham, MD: Rowman & Littlefield.

Goodson, I. (2006) 'The rise of the life narrative', *Teacher Education Quarterly*, 33, 4: 7–21. The notion of narrative learning as employed in this book was first developed by I. Goodson in a paper 'Narrative capital, Narrative learning' written for a course at the University of Barcelona (Mimeo 2005).

—— (2008) *Investigating the Teacher's Life and Work*, Rotterdam & Taipei: Sense.

—— (2010) *Finding Our Story: life politics in the New Age*.

Goodson, I. and Sikes, P. (2001) *Life History Research in Educational Settings: learning from lives*, Buckingham and Philadelphia: Open University Press.

Hoggart, R. (1958) *The Uses of Literacy*, Harmondsworth, Middlesex: Penguin Books in association with Chatto and Windus.

Hopkins, R.L. (1994) *Narrative Schooling*, New York: Teachers College Press.

Houten, C. van (1998) *Erwachsenenbildung als Schicksalspraxis: Grundlagen für zeitgemässes lernen*, Verlag Freies Geistesleben.

McEwan, H. and Egan, K. (eds) (1995) *Narrative in Teaching, Learning and Research*, New York: Teachers College Press.

Polkinghorne, D. (1988) *Narrative Knowing and the Human Sciences*, Albany: SUNY Press.

—— (1995) 'Narrative configuration in qualitative analysis', in J. A. Hatch and R. Wisniewski (eds) *Life History and Narrative*, London: Falmer.

Ranson, S., Martin, J., Nixon, J. and McKeown, P. (1996) 'Towards a theory of learning', *British Journal of Educational Studies*, 44, 1: 9–26.

Ricoeur, P. (1991) 'Life in quest of narrative', in D. Wood (ed.) *On Paul Ricoeur: narrative and interpretation*, London: Routledge, 20–33.

Rogers, C. (1969) *Freedom to Learn: a view of what education might become*, Columbus, OH: Merill.

Rossiter, M. (1999) 'A narrative approach to development: implications for adult education', *Adult Education Quarterly*, 50, 1: 56–71.

Rossiter, M. and Clark, M.C. (2007) *Narrative and the Practice of Adult Education*, Malabar, FL: Krieger.

Tedder, M. and Biesta, G.J.J. (2009[a]) 'What does it take to learn from one's life? Exploring opportunities for biographical learning in the lifecourse', in B. Merrill (ed) *Learning to Change? The role of identity and learning careers in adult education*, Frankfurt am Main: Peter Lang.

—— (2009[b]) 'Biography, transition and learning in the lifecourse: the role of narrative', in J. Field, J. Gallacher and R. Ingram (eds) *Researching Transitions in Lifelong Learning*, London: Routledge, 76–90.

West, L., Alheit, P., Andersen, A.S. and Merrill, B. (eds) (2007) *Using Biographical and Life History Approaches in the Study of Adult and Lifelong Learning: European perspectives*, Frankfurt am Main: Peter Lang.